To [handwritten, partially obscured]
B[...]

love.
Anneth

THE SINGLE MOTHER'S DIARY

Dr. Ava Eagle Brown

AUTHORS PLACE
—PRESS—

Published by Authors Place Press
9885 Wyecliff Drive, Suite 200
Highlands Ranch, CO 80126
AuthorsPlace.com

Manufactured in the United States of America.

ISBN: 978-1-62865-663-3

CONTENTS

INTRODUCTION

About the compiler: Dr. Ava Eagle Brown, author of The Mango Girl, speaker and coach.

DR. AVA EAGLE BROWN

Multi-award-winning International Speaker, Author and Transformation mindset business coach, Dr. Ava Eagle Brown is in a class by herself. Ava coaches, trains and speaks globally to help others shift their mindsets to change their lives and businesses ultimately affecting their bottom-line.

HER CLIENTS INCLUDE:

*HSBC
*London Borough of Merton
*CitiBank Group
*London Borough of Croydon
*West Minister Kingsway College
*Barbados Investment & Development Corporation
*Milewski & Partnerzy- Poland
*Play Time is over -Washington
Barbados Investment & Development Corporation- Barbados
Digicel group - Jamaica
Wise Women's Retreat - Netherlands

Volunteer Work

Ambassador for Evolve Homeless Charity

Mentor to St Pauls Private Girls School - London

She is the author of her memoir *The Mango Girl is* soon to be a feature film plus a documentary titled *"Imagine A World "*., set to be released in 2019.

Ava as well as being a best-selling author has coached hundreds to write their own stories and continues to do so through her book coaching programmes.

Ava has moved from a family who is moderately illiterate a household name globally. *Mindset shift is her biggest Mantra.* She has shared stage with the likes of Levi Roots, Eric Thomas, Nick Vujicic, Hollywood -Sheryl Lee Ralph, Darren Marissa Peer, Joseph McClendon 3rd among others of influential and status in this space.

She has been featured in:

The *Financial Times*

The Sunday Mirror

The BookSellers

Book Brunch

BBC

Huffington Post

London Live

Huffington Post

The Voice Newspaper

Television Jamaica

Sky TV

LBC Radio London

Radio Jamaica

**The Guardian* just to name a few of the press that have sought words from this great country girl turned corporate queen.

Contact : www.avaeaglebrown.com

@avabrown24 twitter

dr.avabrown24 Instagram

PREFACE

When I thought of doing the single mother anthology, it was an exciting feeling, to be honest. I was sitting in my car frustrated, wondering what I would do with my son because of the job offer I was just presented with. But of course, I had no childcare, no family support and we needed the money. You see that has been the story of my own life for the past 18 years.

The job was there, I didn't have anybody to look after my son, and here I was once again. I had fallen back into a situation that I never wanted to be in, again.

That of a single mother.

Before my son (Mikhel Kai) was seven, I had my daughter, Chardonnay; life was hard and we worked together for a long time on this journey, just the two of us juggling life.

I never wanted to be a single mother again, and here I was. What was I supposed to do when my eldest who was now 14, a grown teenager, and I was about to I give birth to a baby? Was I to do an abortion? Was I to die? Trust me, getting an abortion was one thought, but I decided to carry on.

He was a new addition to our family, and I had started doing everything I swore I would never have to do, again.

I was doing the nursing, changing all the diapers and I always thought I would never do all of that alone again, but what was I to do?

Single mothers, as busy as life gets, please remember focussing on what you want is the best way to get out of this space. We sometimes sink into a pit of poor me syndrome, but listen to me, learn to snap out of that space and focus more on what you desire at the end of this chapter of your life.

I was gifted with a beautiful son, a fantastic kid who enriched my life. I never wanted to be a single mother again, and my unique mother journey began when I was at the age of 22. I was married back in 1998 and gave birth to my beautiful daughter, Chardonnay Elizabeth, and didn't do everything alone at first, as her father and I were together. But as life would have it, we got separated, but it was never that challenging, as I was able to afford nannies, etc. Then, life happened again, and I ended up in the UK.

(See The Mango Girl and learn more about my life, as this book isn't so much about that.)

However, life became more challenging when I moved to the UK, and I didn't have any support system. Back in Jamaica, you can ask a neighbour or friend to give you a hand in picking up the child, but here in the UK, the laws are so strict that you can't have anybody pick up the child unless they are registered on a list and it becomes complicated beyond belief.

So, how was I going to juggle everything? As a result, I spent a lot of my time being a supply teacher, who was an agency staff, and so I lived a very cagey and sheltered life, and to be honest, sometimes it was frustrating. I couldn't date, I couldn't get a breather, and I had no personal space most of the time.

I wasn't able to take a breather, yet I found myself caring for two children as a single mother, and struggling with the bills was hard. I found myself wrapping my son in a blanket sometimes in winter due to lack of petrol. Oh, it has been hard. I was bending my back all by myself, and it was draining. I was going for a corporate job and just making enough money to pay for the nursery; his father didn't contribute. Chardonnay became a teenager very quickly, her needs changed, and I wanted to write a book about showing the other side of what single parents go through. I'm not in a position to give you the whole background of my single-parent life, but sometimes I feel like giving up because I feel like the one pair of shoes that gets worn everywhere.

You see my single mum's journey got complicated here in the UK when my daughter was diagnosed with mental health issues, and then, my life became harder because I had to be the one to deal with it all. Her dad, even today, has not come to grips with it and I think it is either he doesn't want to deal with it or doesn't know how to deal with it. So, this meant that I did not just have to carry ALL (Burden), but also, I had a mental health issue added to my pile.

My life became more complicated, and I found myself at the Priory (private mental hospital) a lot for years and also the NHS hospital with my daughter's mental health challenges.

There were days when she would cry like a baby, and I would have to shush her, sing her lullabies and stroke her face, while I sat there crying inside. Sometimes, in the struggle of it all, I realized that the financial piece of my single-mother journey wasn't the hardest, it was the emotional aspects that I found most challenging.

This is one of the hardest things, because a mother should have the answers to fix her child, be able to give them something to make them feel better and be able to make things better instantly. I was helpless about her problems, and I just had to support her in any way possible and be by her side, which was the best I could do.

Therefore, my single mother journey has impacted me terribly.

My life felt like it consisted of school runs and being a taxi service for activities my son attended each week. He loved basketball and karate, which he engaged in regularly. On Saturdays, he visited his friends and on Sundays, he played rugby and also attended church with me. Talking about it without tears welling in my eyes was hard. It was hard to say to my son that I had been trying to prevent him from pursuing something he was genuinely passionate about. He actively wanted to try new things and be a part of something and interact with other children. I think that's the main reason he loved to go to these activities and that made me feel guilty.

I, however, think kids who are exposed to negative parenting are better off in a stable, harmonious one-parent family, more than living in a tumultuous, two-parent family, where kids are exposed to turmoil, arguments, and fits of anger on a regular basis. That was our story, and I didn't want that for my kids.

Although my ex-husband did not live with us, I hated his presence. Ever since he left, it was the best thing he did because it gave me a chance to parent my children the way I wanted to in a safe environment. So, I want you to pause and imagine you are a single mother who is out there questioning yourself. I want you to stop questioning yourself. If this is where you are right now, give your children what they need and the best of you and make them your priority; it will raise your vibration.

So I say to those who are single mothers, regardless of how you got here, you cannot fix it right now. Where you are is where you can step up to the plate and decide that you are going to be the best version of yourself that you can be, even if you were not parented yourself.

So, single mothers out there, I salute you. I'll say to you, be the best version of yourself you can be regardless of what life has thrown at you. Be kind to yourself. You did the best you could do in all of your circumstances and personally, one lesson I have learned is never to carry guilt and shame, and I had to get to a place where I did just that. I left those two things behind me. As a single mother that was hard.

I had two children from different fathers, and I felt ashamed for a very long time. However, I was also given a chance to love them twice as much. To be the best mother I could be. In this state, I learned to listen better to my kids without all the noise and trauma of my ex. Life was more harmonious.

On another positive note, I want to thank my kids for being such amazing children to me, even when I didn't deserve it. I didn't deserve their forgiveness or their patience. I love you, and I thank you. I apologize for all those times I didn't have for you, I didn't deserve your forgiveness, love or even patience. Thanks for being patient with me.

I'm proud to see the woman and man that you are becoming, and it gives me such joy to see you both prosper despite our circumstances. This piece is dedicated to the single women out there; those who are trying to do this, but also to Chardonnay Elizabeth and Mikhel Kai, this is dedicated to you too from my heart. I want to say thank you to the women who showed up in this book. I am going to stand with a van and change the narrative conversation and agenda around a single woman to assure the world that single men don't have to produce worthless children and we don't have to be willing. Also, we don't benefit from the timer and always have to be what society classifies as the less.

The biggest reason for this book is to change the narrative of how single mothers are seen, demonstrating that we can turn out well-measured children who are valuable to the world. I also wanted to have women share their stories to empower others and help them along the way with their own journey

To all the co-authors in this book and all single mamas, know that you are amazing, and you make this earth shine brighter. I'm just so delighted that I got to stand beside you at this particular time in my own path.

If you want to grab a chat about how you can be included in volume 2, please email me today at info@avabrown.org.

FOREWORD

Blamed and shamed, admired and glorified. Being a Single Mum spans these concepts. Sister listen to me, if you are married, cohabiting or in visiting relationship, once a relationship brakes down for whatever reason, we ultimately find ourselves in the rank of 'Single Mums.' Sadly, some women find themselves bereaved with choices being taken away from them. Of course, some fathers choose to play a vital role in their children's lives, while others walk away without a thought.

With all this as single mothers, often we can become a threat for other women who are in a secure relationship.

The fodder for social research, media attention, and society's ills, often lay squarely at our feet, and we face this unexpected change of events in our lives as best we can. It would seem that children in two-parent families are balanced, hardworking, and successful, while the offspring of single mums (whatever the reason) is the root of the problems facing society. It is true that life is so much harder bringing up children with a parent missing, but many of the women were able to draw on healthy family and friendship networks. When the children grow up to create successful pathways for themselves, then we are perceived as super mums.

The complexities of these relationships are explored here by women who have been through and often come from traumatic breakups. Ava Brown, in her inimitable persuasive manner, has called the women in this book to action – to tell their stories, the highs and the lows, the pain and peace, from survival to conquering and overcoming.

We all have a story. I believe that hearing the stories of others' can keep strengthen, heal and free us but also inspire others tell their own stories.

Marva Rollins OBE

ABOUT JOAN ANITA DAVIS-WILLIAMS

Renowned Edupreneur and Edutainer
Association of Supervision and Curriculum
Development (ASCD)

Over Joan's many years of practicing her craft, she has trained over 15,000 teachers in tandem with HEART / NTA, National Youth Service, and Jamaica Teaching Council. She has also developed and implemented programmes for the stakeholders in various educational institutions in Jamaica and many other private and public entities, both locally and abroad. Some such entities in Jamaica are the Bank of Jamaica, National Commercial Bank, Bank of Nova Scotia, Jamaica National Building Society, USAID, Lasco Group of Companies, EDUCOM Credit Union, The Jamaica Teachers Association (J.T.A), The Ministry of Education, Youth and Culture (CSEC workshops and the training of all the lab technicians for the Technical and Vocational areas in schools), some tertiary institutions, such as the University of the West Indies, Mona, University of Technology, The Mico University College and other teacher training colleges, such as Church, G.C Foster, Moneague, Bethlehem Moravian, Shortwood, Sam Sharpe, St. Joseph's, Edna Manley College of the Visual and Performing Arts and College of Agriculture, Science and Education.

Joan has shared a host of voluntary work in developing and implementing custom-designed programmes based on accessed needs with the medical fraternity, homes of safety for children, juvenile centres, adult correctional institutions in her home country Jamaica.

Joan's professionalism and innovativeness have been recognized in multiple areas including, two one-hour segments on the locally televised in-depth programme Profile. The Belize Life Underwriter's Staff Development Workshop participants and the Women's Fellowship of the United Church in Grand Cayman, along with many Jamaicans who have also documented their glowing commendations and the desire for more from this vivacious facilitator. Joan Anita has numerous awards due to the level of professionalism and excellence she puts into her work as an educator. Awards and recognitions received by this phenomenal educator includes:

- Principal's Beyond the Boundaries Awards, Ardenne High School, 2010

- Student Council Award for Outstanding Contribution 2008, Ardenne High School.

- Top students in CSEC Food and Nutrition in Jamaica, 2000-2004 and 2008

- Most Influential Teacher, Student Council Award, Ardenne High School, 2010 and 2011

- Certificate of Appreciation for Faithful Service, Ardenne High School, 2000-2011.

- Outstanding Master Teacher of Jamaica, Jamaica Teaching Council / Ministry of Education 2006 and 2015

- Thirteen years of Outstanding Work Award Ardenne Extension High School 2002

SINGLE MOTHER

"Remember that if you try to push water up hill, it will come back in your face and drown you!" Those words carefully peeled from the lips of my mother as she laid on her stomach in bed, her feet crossed at her ankles, and her hands supporting her chin. This was her only response when I gleefully announced I was going to marry my tall, dark, handsome man whom I met and fell madly in love with at college.

For years these words resonated with me, although I was not sure what they meant.

Papa, on the other hand, echoed as he sat on the edge of the mattress, removing his socks by slowly peeling them from his toes, then his heels, then flashing them to straighten them out. "If you have a pig that was taken from the mud and you bade (bathe) him off, lock him into a glass case for years, any day you forget to close that gate and the pig escapes…straight back to the mud!"

Frankly, I did not understand their parables and I did not seek clarification. Only thing I knew was I was getting married. After all, a college diploma in hand and a husband completes the package.

"Yes, I do." We said this positively on our wedding day, along with some real romantic lines we coined.

"Money that my woman and I have, you nigga, will never live long enough to see it." From the mouth of my husband years after. Yes, I was mindful of the fact that I have been cheated on, left, right and centre, Jamaican term: "I was getting bun!" My father's words came to pass.

"Small bills like those, (mortgage, all utilities), I no longer pay!" From the mouth of my husband.

Also, when he openly showcased his relationship with this rich business lady with whom he lived with, I knew the rumours were true.

By then I was sure I was one of his several women, although his rich mistress thought she was the only woman in his life. While my husband honed his extramarital relationships, I worked at caring for the home, creating extra income and keeping my full-time job as a teacher and mother.

Oh yes, I had to be his 'mistress' on demand, regardless. He tried to dictate how I should dress, what I should eat and what I should prepare for his meals. At home, I had to cater to his vegetarian needs, although I knew he was not practicing such in other places. I played along with his dietary games and made him feel as though he was a vegetarian.

"Dawg who no gaade him yard, caa mek demand pan him owna" In other words: *"If you're not living up to your obligations, you are not privileged to certain things."*

If I had cooperated with the abuses of all types, I would have celebrated 40 'two-faced' years of marriage, July 29, 2018! I am sure I would have lost all my teeth and possibly be in some severe 'man-made' pain, while keeping my pity party. I decided to contribute to the decaying marriage by becoming more quarrelsome and unladylike. Staying in this mess for the sake of my children or what my pastor and parents would say no longer mattered.

I found it difficult managing four children, trying to meet their needs, these were two young boys, months apart by birth and they each had different mothers; these are the kids that were in toe when I met my husband at college.

I was trying to save the house from being sold, securing all the utilities from being disconnected, surviving on a steady diet of chicken cooked in all forms, canned mackerel, sprats (small bony and very cheap fish, then), porridge of all types for all meals and the same outfits for many occasions were daunting.

I credited the very cheap school lunches for the two older boys and our daughter, while I managed to pay the babysitter/helper. Although, I was a trained educator and was fully employed. I honed my craft in many different areas, using all the different areas of my Home Economics training. I was fully satisfied with having my two or three tomatoes for lunch daily at work. I learned long after that many of my colleagues thought I was practicing proper nutrition, hence my choice for lunch.

I was an entrepreneur who sold cooked food in my community and at my workplace; sold clothes I sewed to people locally and abroad and peddled my wares, such as household items, toiletries, and shoes I purchased abroad when I visited for one day. My one-day visit abroad at the end of each month was aimed at completing two days of domestic work in one day, and then shopped for the different items that I would skilfully pack and return home with. In my Jamaican term, I was a 'haggler.'

Parenting all four children meant meeting their needs based on age and gender, guiding some with their schoolwork, while developing their soft skills, and teaching them to do their age-appropriate chores. I played an active role in their school, doing my house duties to ensure all were comfortable, juggling many jobs to put food on the table and paying all the bills. I borrowed from just about everyone I knew.

I also had to juggle supporting my own parents on a monthly basis. and I never missed a month. For many months I had to borrow from others to provide for them. They never had a clue as to what I was going through financially, but emotionally I think they suspected something based on the parables they spoke in my hearing.

In the meantime, my wardrobe was made up of many recycled items. Although I designed and created the most beautiful outfits for both males and females, I could not afford to change our wardrobe as often as I had wanted. However, I became very creative.

I thought that I had heaped all my estranged husband's clothes in his car trunk, unknowingly to him, one afternoon when he visited and went to have a long shower. By this time, he had partially moved out and was living with a rich mistress. However, months later there were still some of his older clothes in a cupboard.

My most gorgeous skirts were made from these 'wat left' pant legs and as time went by, I dyed them various colours.

I also had a particular pair of shoes that were made from 'Burlap' (a thick and loosely woven fabric) and I took pleasure in dyeing them different colours as well.

A number of my colleagues knew my tactics, and so when it rained, they made sure to alert me that I should remain upstairs for a while. Imagine my clothes and shoes 'bleeding' in the rain!

I was often complimented about my dress and deportment. If only they all knew. "When trouble tek you pickney shut fit you" (When your back is 'against the wall,' or you are in serious trouble, then you have to seek the best and fastest solutions without compromising your integrity). I was happy when my daughter Kamika and I could share outfits.

T.G. benefitted from my dyeing skills because for his graduation from primary to high school, I changed his khaki pants to black, while I carefully sewed his white shirt and tie. He cleaned and wore his old school shoes. I was happy that the weather that day remained overcast. I was summoned to court because my estranged husband wanted full custody of the four children. However, I was reminded by the court that I had no right to 'fight' for his two boys, and I should concentrate on my two, Kamika, aka Kamy and Tèion, aka T.G.

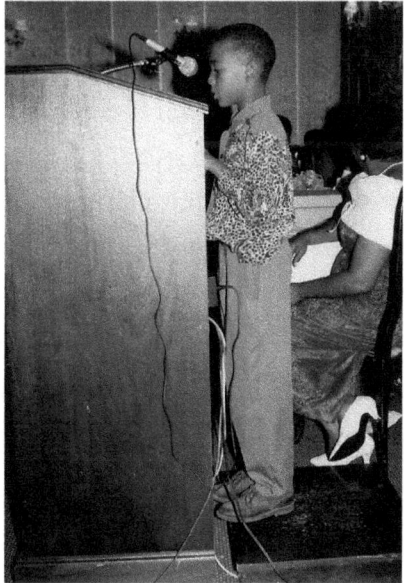

WITH GOD'S HELP

I had teary eyes the first morning T.G. was getting ready to attend high school because together we fumbled at trying to tie his school tie.

At that point I was angry that his father was not around to assist him on this special occassion. T.G went across to my neighbours who assisted him. Thank God, by the said afternoon he was able to do his tie on his own.

"It surely was not easy raising this son!" I could have raised four others with the energy I expended raising him.

As a single mother raising children, especially a boy, was extremely challenging. It was a real hit and miss for me at times. So far things are looking great. I am pleased with the products God has shaped. A mother is not a father and cannot be one. Therefore, I tried not to be one. Instead, I aligned my children with positive families with great male role models for them to emulate and to know what should be expected.

Speaking only positives into my children's lives and empowering them happened often, but there were times when I did the opposite. This was not good! To date, there are proofs of lovely letters and cards expressing my love, or of sharp reprimands that I have sent to them in various stages of their lives. At age 16, Kamika read me a letter I wrote to her on her 9th birthday. T.G. still mounts one written to him a few years ago in his room. Although, I was a hurting and bitter single mother, I tried very hard not to compare my children with others, whether among siblings or their peers.

However, sadly at times, I found myself labelling my son with the negative traits of his father. I must confess that it was easy to see the despicable habits of my husband in my young son more quickly than his good characteristic.

I spoke to my son as if I was talking to his father! My children were given their responsibilities based on their ages and competencies. They started hand washing their underwear by age four (without knowing I was assisting) and my son's hand washed and ironed their khaki uniforms at the age of ten. At age twelve my son's responsibility was to ensure that there was always bread in the house for his family.

He had to save a portion of his lunch money and purchase bread when needed. He consumed much less bread after the responsibility was given. Once he blundered and instead of purchasing bread for his family, he bought a pizza and drink for himself during lunchtime at school. There was no bread, and we kept our silence. The silence was broken one Saturday morning with a long letter I wrote to him. I used the opportunity to kindly remind him about the importance of a man keeping his promise to his family, regardless. As my support, I used a number of relevant Bible verses to 'drive' out my points.

I always seized the teachable moments because my focus was to help my children realise that independence and responsibility go together. I never compromised and I tried to practice what was right. I was not liked at times, but I did not care! When T.G. lost his Math book the first month of the first form in high school, I made him save his lunch money and purchase a new book. As a responsible mother, I ensured he got a healthy breakfast and dinner.

My mother thought I was wicked and said I should have flogged him and then replaced it! Oh no! He had to make some sacrifices as I did and that was more effective. He learnt his lesson well. Doing things to impress people and to win my children's favour was a 'no no' for me. I had to practice balance and resisted the desire to be too lenient or too harsh with my children because of their father's absence and dirty practices. Giving up or giving in were not options! Finding my children's strength's and talents and supporting them as much as possible helped.

I celebrated my children's achievements, however simple and trying and I attended all functions or activities in which they were involved and that boosted their self-esteem. They were involved in clubs and church. Although I was a tired, low budget wardrobe, single parent without a vehicle of my own; I found the time to attend and remained at all their rehearsals and functions. I started attending church with them later as well.

"Train up a child in the way he should go but be sure you go that way yourself." Charles Spurgeon. Talking with my children as often as possible and not to them, allowed me to get feedback, which assisted me to continue or change course. Some feedback was harsh! "Hard pill to swallow!"

We shared ideas, asked opinions, and discussed different aspects of life. Our discussions were not limited to schoolwork. I paid keen attention to any harmful behaviour being developed and sought help to deal with them. For example, stealing, lying, bullying, low self-esteem, smoking etc. I never ridiculed them during or after the dealing of the situations. Although, I was not from a single parent home, I ensured that some of my parents parenting skills were never practised in my home.

"MI FRITEN BAD" (I WAS ALARMED OR FRIGHTENED)

One Saturday morning T.G and I were watching a documentary about the effects of smoking on your health. After watching the gruesome graphics, my six-year-old son commented, *"I am really happy I quit smoking!"*

I was astonished, but I kept my composure. Upon inquiring, he shared with me that this habit was developed when he accompanied Kamika and I to Kamika's dance classes on Saturday mornings at the Little Theatre. He said he often picked up the cigarette 'buts' discarded by the adults and smoked them. I did not realise this because a vendor usually gave him an icy mint to camouflage the smell on his breath. If I had known!!! Wicked woman!!

"AGAIN!"

T.G. and I were in snail traffic one morning on our way to Ardenne High School when suddenly we came to a long pause on West Kings House Road at the stop lights. We were many cars away from the front.

As we gazed around while biding time, I noticed him paying close attention to a young man on the sidewalk kneading some leafy substance resembling ganja in his palm. When the young man finished this detailed activity, he rolled his 'spliff' then moistened the edges to ensure it was sealed. With great satisfaction plastered on his face, he pleasantly looked at it and gingerly pinched off one end of the 'spliff,' which he carelessly dropped beside him, then placed the other end in his mouth. All during this time, T.G.'s eyes were glued to the young man. We started to move slowly away from this scene.

T.G. rearranged himself in his seat, hissed his teeth and mumbled, "Idiot, he put the wrong part in his mouth." My curiosity peeked! My son was only fourteen years of age and was about to enter the fifth form! I found out weeks after that T.G. was indeed smoking 'ganja.'

No wonder he hurriedly got home before I did in the evenings and I noticed his sleeping pattern had changed. His lips had become much dryer, and he was consuming a lot of water. Why was he falling asleep in classes, even in my classes, I wondered? Nobody sleeps in my class! One night I was so upset that my high-pitched conversation ended with me chasing him through the bushes and down to the community centre because he insisted that he was not involved in smoking marijuana.

I took him to my Iridologist. She uncovered his habits, although he tried taking 'God off the cross' and insisting that he was not smoking marijuana. He told the doctor that a large amount of smoke she saw in his lungs had to do with the area in which he lives. He further stated that a lot of people in his community smoke and he might have inhaled some.

T.G. told me years after that he quit the habit based on how I handled it. I did not bash him or 'crucifie' him, but instead, I spoke with him. Thank God for having reminded me of my past as a child. Seek to build cooperation with your children and avoid being controlling. Desist from taking part in power struggles. Try to know their friends and their families. You might not always succeed, but show interest in who your child is involved with. Ensure you understand who their role models are.

A fatherless child will sometimes seek out others to affirm him/her. Observe your children and see what and whom they admire. If the father is alive, responsible and accessible, have your children spend valuable time with him. It hurts, but I chose their father, and they are not accountable.

I tried to live a decent life before God so my children could use my habits and values as a part of their experiences. Encourage your children to be sensible and educated. I thank God for Northern Caribbean University because they cleaned up my son and guided him to know more about Jesus Christ. As a single parent, I avoid being overprotective or too permissive, therefore, setting limits helped.

Giving my children material things as a form of compensation was not practised, but instead, I gave them love and made them understand from the beginning that they will have to be satisfied with what I have to offer.

Téion was about thirteen years old when he started acting up and was making some financial demands of me. He wanted a new pair of jeans, and I could not afford it. Although it was not a name brand jean and one of the cheapest type, I could not afford it. I tried to explain my circumstances, but he did not seem to understand. After all, at thirteen he was now comparing styles etc. with his peers.

Things were getting tough and I came to the conclusion that 'Enough was enough'! So the following month I gathered all the bills, handed him my pay cheque and told him to pay all the bills from my cheque. I also told him to take the rest of the money and buy whatever he wanted. I went to bed and left him budgeting. In the wee hours of the morning, he was still at it. He then said in a humbling tone, "Mommy, how do you do it?" That activity helped. Many times he handed me the money he saved to assist in the home.

Another knee jerker was a movie I watched with him in which the mother stole to support her children. She was imprisoned, and during her stay, she was abused by the other inmates. The children were separated and sent to different foster care homes. They too were abused.

My son wept uncontrollably and promised not to ask for 'things.' He was in a sober mood for quite a while. That helped me tremendously. To date, my son is not hyped about name brand clothes.

Here are some advice tips I lived by. Be careful not to spoil your son by not allowing him to help with the chores in the home. Don't be guilty of producing a spoilt man who sees women as helpers. Prevent your son from being embarrassed or 'used' when he becomes an adult. Women respect men much more when they are not 'housework handicaps.'

Demonstrate the common courtesies, so your children can pattern you. Take them out to experience fine dining and to plays or movies from which they can learn. Invest in positive reading material. Help them see positive things in action.

When age appropriate and in stages, show them pictures of sections of naked people, so it quells their curiosity. This way they will not be tempted to get into promiscuous situations because he is overly curious.

As a mother I allowed my son to see parts of my naked body at different stages of his life. He was never appalled. My daughter was older than her brother so she saw his growth in steps.

Teach your son how to wash his penis and your daughter her vagina. Demonstrate how to practice good hygiene. Never forget to pray with and for your children. There is **power in prayer.**

A.J Packer said, *"The weaker we feel, the harder we lean. And the harder we lean, the stronger we grow."*

"ME A GO MAD."

Sometimes I felt as if I was going out of my mind. However, T.G. always reminded me to take it easy. How could I when he was a source of most of my concern? I had many sleepless nights and wondered what his future would be.

One day T.G. came to me and said, *"Mommy feel my breasts,"* I did and then he continued, *"See I have no lumps. See Mommy, I am stress free."*

Before, I used to complain about the lumps in my breasts that hurt, especially when I'm under stress, and this was very often. My son knew then that he was a source of most of my pain.

Frankly, from that day forward, I turned everything over to Jesus and started to pray more. No more pain in my breasts. As a single parent, you can be burnt out to take time to pamper yourself. Take a 'chill pill.' Remain positive and try and create a good sense of humour.

Join a support group for single parents and call on trusted loved ones, friends and neighbours for help. Do not remove yourself from your child and 'bundle' yourself in a corner. Get out and find new hobbies. Talk about your problems with positive people. Avoid depressing ones.

Over the years T.G has helped me strengthen my spiritual walk further. He gave me Psalm 51 verse 10 "Create in me a clean heart o Lord, and renew a right spirit within me." because he thought I was too 'bitter' and harboured too much toxicity. He has shown me how to forgive and let go. He does not keep malice, he is not judgmental, and he has a high level of integrity.

About three years ago, T.G called me from a car park saying, "Mummy, I am watching a lady and possibly her son. I am smiling because they remind me of both of us. The young man had to open the car door for the lady, he went ahead, opened and held the door to the pharmacy. He even had to retrieve something that fell from her hurriedly. Thank you, mummy."

After 39 and 33 years, both my children are making me proud. My son promised never to leave his wife and son as he was far too aware of what I went through.

As a husband and father he has a problem to grasp how his father walked out on him when he was only one year old. Kamika is doing a super mom's job and I am so grateful to see how they have both turned out.

They have both raised their children under the fear of the Lord. I credit my parenting style to learning from the mistakes that I saw in so many of my students relationships with their parents. During and out of classes I entertained ideas from my students about best and inferior methods of their parents/guardians.

I developed and facilitated a series of parenting sessions that have benefitted hundreds of adults.

God has been good.

KEY LEARNING

God is the source and without him, I would be a failure as a single mother- Jeremiah 29 v 11 was my guided scripture

Having taught at the female prison for seven years that has guided my decisions for doing harm to my ex.

My interaction with other children from single parent homes and how they were handled, pointed me to stay clear of parenting that way

As an educator, I had to make a great job of it as I knew my story was one that others were learning from.

Joan A. Davis-Williams

Edutainer and Edupreneur.

ABOUT CHRISTIANAH AGBABIAKA

I was born in Kwara State, Nigeria in the '80s to Yoruba parents. I've lived most of my life in London when my parents decided to relocate to the UK.

I grew up in East London, a very multi-cultured environment, which has taught me so much about different communities. I'm proud to state that I am raising my awesome little human in the same environment that I grew up in.

Since then, I've had the pleasure of working or studying in the areas of fashion retail, fashion PR, journalism, events, hosting, voice-acting, charity fundraising, marketing, HR admin, business management and recruitment.

In most recent years, I've focused my work on coaching, career & employment, learning & personal development, a passion for psychology and a self-taught mental health & well-being advocate, and currently a trainee counsellor and working towards completing my qualifications.

In my spare time when I'm not working, I can be found at home dancing with my daughter, making crafts and baking. Also, at the gym, museums, art galleries, music gigs and literary events.

A LABOUR OF LOVE

INTRO

My parenting journey started 8 years ago when I became pregnant at age 27 and guess what I wasn't expecting it!!!! Life was going by and I was a normal African girl at the prime of my life living in the greatest city of the world and a child was the furthest thing from my mind. At the age of 16, I was incredibly confident that I didn't want to become a mother at any stage of my life and guess what? I became a mother despite this!

So how did this happen? Well, there was a nice man and I was depressed. Let's just say I was struggling in all aspects of my life at the time and was extremely vulnerable. My self-awareness and self-worth were low, and so were my senses and sensibilities. It happened pretty quickly, and I knew what I had to do.

I was living at home with my folks, but that wasn't the problem. It was the economic downturn, there was not much work for me, and I had become a student again-studying undergraduate in Public Relations. I found this challenging to fund, having been at the University some years previous and I had exhausted what I would have been entitled to. Family and friends helped, but this compounded my problems when I fell into a wellbeing deficit. I slipped hard and was drowning. I could not support myself, but I had a roof over my head. My parents didn't mind, but I cared. I should have been looking after them and it depressed me.

I had failed at a relationship before this time, I was even engaged, but it was a long-distance romance, and I didn't have my families blessing. Besides, he may not have loved me genuinely, that may have been a lucky escape. The point is I was broken by it and incredibly lonely. Nothing felt great in my life, and I fell into a major depressive state.

So, I met a nice man, who distracted me from my problems. Well, let's say it wasn't a romance, but we got involved very quickly, and then I fell pregnant equally as fast. As I said, I had lost my sense and sensibilities.

That nice man wasn't very nice as soon as I told him I was pregnant and that I would make my own choices regarding moving forward with a baby. At the time I was pregnant with my daughter, my parents wanted to look after me, but I could not continue living under their roof. As I had lived away from home prior and been mature enough, they encouraged me to start carving a path to manage my life, my child and my home.

Eventually, I ended up in a temporary flat, not too far away from my family, and I was able to settle in. I struggled with going to work in my first trimester; I was severely anaemic and dehydrated, as I couldn't keep food down. I worked with a boutique firm in Canary Wharf, but every time I was there, I just wasn't present. In my head, I felt so overwhelmed, there was so much to do, I mean I was going to be a Mum, and I was figuring out how on earth I was going to make it all work.

When I was about 5months expectant, I got a call around 10 pm from the Police station in Forest Gate. They said they had that 'not so nice man' with them and described him as my partner, but he really wasn't, and I told them so. It turned out he had been arrested for various types of fraud. It was a shock to his family/friends. The police put him on the phone and the biggest mistake I made at that moment was agreeing to speak with him. I was calm and understood precisely what was going on, but I was screaming inside. I had so many questions, but yet, I just spoke calmly and listened to everything. I knew then that he was going to be a lot more trouble than he was worth.

That was eight years ago, and I have such a purpose because of that child. She's now a super amazing little mini-me. I'm so grateful for her; she may have saved my life!!

Has it been a comfortable journey for her and I? No, it has been a labour of love!

THE BATTLE

I had this healthy and beautiful girl, although the hospital wasn't a great experience for me, it was a miracle. I had her via emergency Caesarean, born on a Saturday afternoon in the local hospital in the summer of 2010, with my mother by my side. I returned to my parent's home to be cared for by my mother. I had my family to look after us, particularly my mother. I was a child again having become a first-time mother. I took to mothering pretty well, being the eldest in my sibling group sibling found it easier as I was accustomed to looking after children even as a child. Apart from the overwhelming feeling of "Oh my, I'm responsible for this little person for the rest of her life." It was scary, but it was an honest mission.

I found myself going through the court system often. Due to the fact that my daughters' Father decided that his route to be the best father was to lie and play victim to remain in the country. It was challenging and no one wanted to talk about the issue of immigration or how/what/who people do to get what they need.

He played dirty, and it shocked me, he was accusing my parents and I of blackmail and stopping him from seeing our daughter. This was wholly untrue, and it stung me to the core that he could drag my family into it when they had shown him nothing but kindness -though he didn't deserve it.

It took me too many lows, and I struggled under this strain. Enjoying the parent and baby classes, the park, trips away, family time, and the milestones of my growing toddler-NO it was taken from us! I even believe it hindered my daughter's original speech abilities. Friends felt further away, and there were only a few people I stayed connected to who have remained with me on this journey to this very day. I still feel so incredibly guilty about that time- I suffered emotionally, and perhaps my daughter did as well.

Two years' worth of court, knowing that not everything stated was the truth, I conceded that I was doing this for my daughter, so I went through the motions and came out the other side ensuring my daughter was the priority. In the long run, I've possibly earned his respect as her mother, which I didn't care for. I'm not sure I could offer the same just yet.

And so it goes...

Today, at age 36, I have continued to grow on that purpose, fighting my demons all the way and having small victories.

I had always intended to work, but I didn't have a job I could go back to once my daughter was born.

I had to start again, and volunteering was my avenue. My daughter was now eligible for a half-day placement in nursery and I used this opportunity to use those hours to grow in my education and my job search. As I had completed a qualification in teaching English as a foreign language, I approached the local Children's Centre who was very instrumental in aiding the contact between the daughter and her father. I had built a good relationship with the staff. I approached and said I'd like to help people as well. I became the poster girl for language and communication working with individual adults who were under vulnerable circumstances. I was boosting their confidence and their language skills and empowered them to improve upon this.

It was around this time that I caught a bug; I wanted to help people, including those closest to me.

I later met someone from a dating site, and we began an almost three-year relationship and I had incredible growth with this gentleman. He was flawed, but so was I. I was also proud to be a mother, but existing as a girlfriend as well. It was friendly and safe.

It was also the time I decided I knew I wanted to be a counsellor. I couldn't figure out how I was going to get there. I'm still not sure as it's been a lonely journey, but I'm several steps closer.

CURRENT SITUATION

I've been through so many transitions; the rise of Universal Credit, unemployment, almost losing our home, two of my younger siblings marrying, my parents' health deviation and being bullied in the workplace by other senior women. The latter had really challenged my confidence in the workplace in general, but also challenged me to find my way and where I truly wanted and needed to be. Counselling was going to be the escape plan. I found this flexibility and freedom of genuinely doing something I am passionate about. Helping others was going to help me!

I am working full time, my daughter is thriving at school, and I am at my strongest, emotionally and mentally. However, I have to work more on my physical and general health. I'm a mother, a daughter, sister, friend and perhaps a girlfriend again one of these days.

I know there are many rivers to cross; some of it may be easy, while some may be hard. I may have to swim for my life, but I do know with my belief and the right people around me, I will press on, I will love, I will be loved, I will grow because it's a labour of love.

KEY LEARNING

My child is only going to be a percentage of me to a certain extent, the rest has to be 100% her.

I'm still learning on the job; I can't expect my daughter to be perfect.

I need to relax and enjoy my child more, they grow so quickly.

ABOUT AVA PAYNE

Ava Payne was conceived in St Kitts, West Indies, and born in London, England. She is a survivor of divorce, homelessness and a failed business venture. Today she is the proud single parent of four beautiful children. Having managed to secure a roof over their heads, Ava has aspirations to use her life experience to embark upon an entrepreneurial career, to remove the barriers stopping potential foster carers (people who care for others who are vulnerable) from embarking on this worthwhile life choice.

Graduating as a mature student was one of her greatest achievements. The determination, sacrifices and challenges along the way made it possible. Ava was the first of her nine siblings to attend a university and obtained a degree in IT and education. She had long been the go-to person for family, friends and colleagues, on all things IT, legal or financial. Ava's naturally inquiring and inquisitive persona makes her excel at investigative tasks. She borrows from her father's mantra, 'You don't have to speak, just because you have a mouth.' Following his guidance, she likes to speak from a position of knowledge, which leads to a lot of fact-finding exercises. The flip side of this is the quest for perfection – which she now knows is not always necessary and can stunt progress.

Her role models are her mother and father (deceased), happily married, hardworking and supportive of their children's ambitions. No, it wasn't easy to leave the Caribbean and come to the motherland. Raising a large family in the '60s in England was no easy task.

But somehow my parents found a way to make their marriage work and have since celebrated their 50th Wedding anniversary. There was never a cross word exchanged between them and whether consciously or unconsciously, Ava wanted to be just like them.

AVA PAYNE STORY

FROM MRS. TO MS.

INTRODUCTION

It's the year 2000, a new millennium, a thousand years have gone, and the start of the next thousand to come. I am entering my fourth decade. I am a Mrs. and happy with my idyllic family life. I am graduating as a mature student from The University of East London I secured a job working in corporate finance in the city. I am a mother – but the struggle to produce a live birth left me emotionally drained and physically exhausted and took seven long years to come to fruition. In spite of this in my mind, the future looked positive as I was the proud parent of a ten-year-old daughter who meant the world to me. I affectionately referred to her as my number one child. Not to negate all those who did not make it into this world, but because this is where I put her in my life. After fighting so hard to get her here, I saw it as my absolute duty to do everything in my power to keep her safe, nurture her and ensure that she was given every opportunity to be the best that she could be. However, I did not know that someone had a different plan for me, and that this year actually started the beginning of the end. The road I was about to travel on was way different from the one I had envisioned

Coming from a large family, I was conscious of my daughter's status as the only child. Our efforts to provide a sibling ended up with the same heartache endured before her birth. She gravitated to her numerous cousins for company and orchestrated sleepovers here and there at every available opportunity. In my stoic fashion, I made a conscious decision to move onto plan B. With this in mind, I looked into the possibility of adding to the family by way of fostering, and if it worked out, moving on to the permanence of adoption. I remember people telling me, "You are so brave!" I did not know what they meant. To me, it seemed like a reasonable, logical step given our circumstances. I could give a home and much-needed love to another child, while making my family complete.

By the end of 2001 I was approved as a foster care guardian and the family has increased by the inclusion of my second daughter, C2 aged 8 joined C1, a treasure and a test all rolled into one. Now I know what they meant! Although the girls bonded immediately, it is anything but comfortable to parent a child of the state. While I saw her as my own, constrictions of the rules and regulations of the local council and the corporate parent, made it a challenge. Simple decisions as to what you can and can't do are wrapped up in discussions with social workers, lots of form filling and attendance at court, supporting formal care plans for the child were all part and parcel of my new role as a foster carer. Although I knew the reasoning for it, it was a complicated process to work with and was hated by the child. She merely wanted to be healthy. As the trials and tribulations evolved, I decided, in 2003, to give up full-time work to be available to support my children. This led to me being in the right place at the right time, to take in my foster son, aged two. As an emergency placement, he was only meant to be with me for a short while. Fast-forward six months and he was still with me when I received the call to accommodate another male foster child J1 aged 10.

As a family of 6, we settled into healthy family life, notwithstanding the intervention of social services and interactions with members of the children's birth families. The children are engaged in girls and boys brigade, Saturday school, and football and swimming lessons. The mum taxi is at full pelt, but it is great to see them grow and embrace different life experiences. Holidays to Malaga and St Lucia also allowed them to see diverse parts of the world firsthand. As a couple, we decided to stabilise the future of C2 and T1 by adopting them. Unfortunately, the corporate parent agreed that for the newly formed family to bond, J1 must be removed from us, and it is standard procedure that we would not be allowed to foster any other children for two years.

Therefore, amid this upheaval, I realised my marriage was over due to the fact my partner and I wanted very different things from a marriage. Now my mind is going into overdrive. How did that happen? What should I do? How will the children cope? The aching heart and flowing tears are symptoms of the place I found myself. It was a very dark private place that no one could see. To the outside world, I was my happy, cheerful self, and with the children, I was still on their case to get homework and chores done as usual; it was a constant balancing act. I was determined that they did not suffer because of the decisions of the adults around them. It was a strain, and I knew I could not function on this level indefinitely and sought help from medical professionals.

It was a bit of a shock when I explained my situation and the doctor declared, "You are suffering from severe depression." My first thought was 'What!? – Am I now officially a crazy lady?' Such was my lack of understanding of mental health issues. The doctor wanted to prescribe pills at first, which I resisted as I am anti-pills. Instead, I opted for the therapy route to get me through the grieving process and anger I felt. As a usually reserved person, group therapy seemed like a route outside of my comfort zone. However, after attending the first group, I was able to put my issues into perspective, and it made me realise that many people are going through 'stuff' that is a lot worse than mine in comparison. The Cognitive Based Therapy helped me focus on my reactions and thoughts about events, rather than focusing on the behaviour of other people. When I finished the treatment, I was now equipped with how to handle depression and various techniques that would be crucial to my survival.

I know it is not for everyone, but I found it good to talk and make sense of the situation. My advice would be to have an open mind and not dismiss the help if you want to move on.

The decade ended after a year-long mediation process to unpick the life we created over the past twenty plus years. Discussions were had regarding finance, assets, and day-to-day living arrangements for the children. Again, it all seemed very civil, but the battle lines were well and truly drawn. Reaction from friends and family were mixed, some taking sides, a few in the middle and others dropped off my radar totally. Numerous solicitors' appointments and court hearings culminated in various legal documents and the long-awaited Decree Absolute. For me, I wanted to maintain continuity in the children's lives and reassure them that no matter what had happened between the adults, they didn't have to pick a side, as we both remain their parents.

NEXT STEP

A new chapter starts, the ring was gone, I was no longer a wife, but I retained the title of Mrs, for the time being. Part of my reasoning for that was I wanted to remain connected to the children. Bearing in mind, I had just given two of them my married name. It seemed wrong somehow to go off and change mine. Another motive is the social stigma attached to being a single mother and having to explain why the names are different. I felt that my status had somehow been reduced now that I was on my own. I had often been told how lucky I was to be happily married and how jealous others were of me. I was consumed by shame and pride and to be honest, it took a long time to let many know of my changed circumstances. I was not ready to change the status quo.

The children seemed to take it in their stride, but looking back I'm not so sure. There were issues at school, and I was called in more than once to sort out various behavioural issues and misdemeanours. However, I question whether they would have come up anyway regardless of the change to the family situation. In fairness, I did not always face these challenges alone. I resolved to be consistent and take practical steps to see them through. Although I kept him in the loop, 'wait till your father gets home' was never part of my action plan. It is hard but necessary to discipline my kids alone but I was firm yet fair and reinforced more their positive behaviour than the negatives ones, I think this was very effective to my kids. was going through a healing process, and it would have been easy to take it out on the children. Instead, I concentrated on the mind-set that I needed to keep in moving forward –for the love of a child!

Adapting to the challenges of my new single parent role, made me stronger and more resourceful. I got plans drawn up to alter the house so everyone could have their own room. The next-door neighbour, who had already extended his home, came to my home and told me I couldn't carry out this extension. In his opinion, I would fill mine with dysfunctional foster children and bring the neighbourhood down! He knew I was now on my own and tried to intimidate me. When I didn't concede to his demands, he garnered the help of the other neighbours by drawing up a petition, which he asked all non-black neighbours to sign. Well, it worked, to a certain extent; the plans were only partially approved by the council. As the extra bedrooms were vetoed, I moved swiftly on to Plan B. Serendipity played its part, as within weeks I secured a lovely new family house. One of the positives was that the girls now each had their own room and space to develop individually. I was used to managing the family finances, but it was challenging maintaining the lifestyle we had become accustomed to on a reduced income, as I wasn't working. After a while, I was lucky enough to find part-time work at a school, which was perfect for supporting my family, as I was home at the end of the school day and off during school holidays.

My role as a Teaching Assistant at my son's school, was fulfilling and gave me a sense of purpose, as I worked with children in small groups to help bring them up to speed. It was strange how work imitated life, as my son was in one of my groups and we both struggled with what hat to wear. I had to be sure not to treat him differently than the others, and he had a few slips calling me mum, instead of Miss. After a time, I was given extra duties and responsibilities that I relished. Although, receiving the role of EAL (English as an Additional Language) TA, came as a bit of a shock – I only speak English! However, failure was not an option. I made use of my IT skills and researched tools to help me succeed. I discovered the wonderful world of Google translates and invested in an iPad to take it with me into the classroom.

As a union member, I started to become more active and was elected as the workplace representative. When a secondment opportunity became available, I jumped at the chance to work full-time in the union office. It was a steep learning curve, accompanied by a comprehensive, structured training programme that prepared me for the role. In my role as a union representative, I found myself supporting members, now negotiating with heads of council departments, Head teachers and Senior Management and various organisational leaders.

CEO of Academy's and HR Consultants. It is an understatement to say I was extremely pleased when I was successful, in my first case, in getting a member reinstated to her post after a suspension and the threat of dismissal loomed on the horizon.

LEAP OF FAITH

It was 17 years into the millennium and I was beginning to believe that the worst was now over. I had done my best for the children; C1 was working full-time as a bus driver and pursuing her dream to be a DJ. C2 was studying at the university to be a mechanical engineer, and T1 was finding his way while in his last year of school. I was delighted by what we have achieved together. Having the label of being part of a single parent family does not have to define us. Being fair and consistent saw us through. By being present and finding a way to laugh and joke, created rounded individuals. Instilling values, standards and manners, equipping them with the skills to get through life is an achievement to be proud of. As I had survived this testing period, I prepared to return to my fostering vocation and help other children along their path.

Just when I thought I had things under control, I was hit by a series of unfortunate events. My landlord of 7 years wanted to sell the house. No problem, I will just get another one! So I did. I could only find a four bed, so C1 didn't move with us and therefore, I would have the spare room to foster. I asked my new landlord for an electricity certificate for the house, but he refused to supply one. I went through the fostering assessment, which for reasons out of my control took almost a year. The final stage was the certificate, so I commissioned the report myself. I presented it to my landlord on the 23rd of December, outlining the work he needed to do. I was shocked to receive a section 21 Notice to evict me on the 2nd of January.

I thought that my protected status as a foster care guardian would make me a priority for housing. I applied and was rejected, the landlord took me to court, and I lost, six months later I was homeless. I found myself and my kids in a small hotel room with 2 -bed and as a result I had to sleep with my children.

It was crammed and inconvenient as and the sink was in arms reach of the beds. How did I end up hear I heard myself say or ask?

The government deemed this OK for me to share a room and bed with my adopted children. We were eventually moved to a two-bed flat in a converted office block in the middle of an industrial estate – excellent – and still I had to share a room with my daughter! Oh, what a journey I tell you.

I had never missed a payment, took good care of the house and did not break my agreement. I was shocked and infuriated. It was so sudden but my wish to help others came true and at that point started to turn my life around.

I had faith that this was not to be my portion and worked tirelessly to highlight my dilemma with the help of my local MP Siobhain McDonagh. She was brilliant in taking my case to parliament and making Theresa May answer to her. The media took up my plight and challenged the council. I am grateful for all the help and exposure I received that resulted in me being rehoused with a spare room to foster.

My story is not an invite to a pity party, for it is the path I have travelled. Haven has been removed in no uncertain terms from my comfort zone. I had to revaluate my journey and myself. It was in the midst of this upheaval that I decided to revert to my original surname and become a Ms. Payne, it was a struggle as I had to almost reprove that I had this surname prior.

However, at the time rebirthing me felt right., as the phoenix rises from the ashes, I am emerging with new strength and purpose to be who I was meant to be.

To all the single mothers out there, believe that resurrection is possible. Be brave and ask for help when you need it, as endings can also be the beginning.

KEY LEARNING

- If I didn't have faith, I would not be the person I am today.
- The truth about, 'It's not you, it's me." Really means in my case, I don't have to live my life as a charade to fit society's expectations.
- The role I play as a single parent cannot be paid for in hard cold cash. I accept payment in laughter, tears, hugs and kisses.
- I was me before I was a mama and will continue to be me when the chicks fly the nest. I will be content knowing I have done the best job I could.

As a Christian, I believe in God. I was brought up in church and brought my children up to the same way.

I appreciate that this way of life is not for everyone. However, the teachings and scriptures of the bible have formed the backdrop to my life for as long as I have known. They have planted me in good stead. It is ironic that I am closing this chapter, which is a snapshot of my journey, by giving credit to the force that knows me best - Psalm 139 describes it better than I can. In essence, it says all the journeys I have been through were pre-ordained and written in my book before my life began! I am comforted by thoughts of someone being there for me, guiding and comforting, making me into the particular unique person that I am. Even when things are not going quite right and I question why certain things happened and others didn't. I accept that these times don't last forever and everything happens for a reason. Thanks are to God.

ABOUT MARVA ROLLINS

Marva Rollins OBE is in her 24th year of Headship. She is in her 19th year as head teacher of Raynham Primary (880 pupils aged 2 - 11), in Edmonton, North London. She was previously head of a junior school in Newham. Marva has a firm commitment to giving children in inner-city schools an opportunity to excel. She has been the recipient of three awards, which recognise her contribution to education and the community. An honorary degree from the original College of Teachers, the Wind rush Education Champions and in January 2017, an OBE for her contribution to Education. In 2009, Marva was named by the Evening Standard as one of the 1,000 most influential people in London, and in 2011, featured in the Metro's top 50 Black Heroes. Recently Marva reduced her time as a head teacher to three days a week and has set up Rollins Education Consultancy Ltd with the foci of supporting and strengthening the leadership of other schools. Preparing future leaders for successful interviews – confidence building and all aspects of the complex interview process, as well as motivating, coaching and mentoring.

Marva has been an active member of the community for nearly 40 years and is a founding member of several community groups including: The Sickle Cell Society, East London Black Women Organisation (ELBOW) and Newham African Caribbean Centre. She is currently a trustee of the Success Club Charity, which works with students in schools and the community on Motivation and Mindfulness. She is a qualified Coach and Mentor, a regular conference speaker, trainer and facilitator in education.

Marva has been one of the lead persons on two essential programmes for BME teachers. She has been Investing in Diversity and Equal Access and playing a pivotal role in increasing the percentage of BME leaders in the UK. Both these programmes have empowered many BME teachers/Deputy head teachers to challenge the status quo, enhance their skills/knowledge and achieved their aims.

Marva is the mother of 3 adult sons and is a grandmother. Sojourner Truth is one of her role models, and she considers the Special Olympics motto, "Lord, let me win, but if I cannot win let me be brave in the attempt."

WHO WOULD IMAGINE? FROM VICTIM TO SUPER HERO?

Being a single parent can come across as a life-limiting condition. Being a parent (albeit in a two-parent family) brings compromises, and we who were on our own had to make a few more.

Being a single parent is not a unique way of being and cannot be defined by a set of given statements.

Yet, the image of a single parent is often seen as a woman at some point in her relation/marriage, has had horrendous experiences.

These experiences have led her to be left on her own to bring up one or more children. When we surface as successful individuals, we are then portrayed as some superhero that has survived and overcame some barriers that others admire.

I was not alone – a few of my friends/family members, were in relationships that are still intact today, but somehow, I ended up with a group of friends who shared my experiences. We have all, to some degree, took our lessons by the horns and got on with life. For some, the challenges are enormous and overwhelming and deserve all the support they need. Some of us were naïve and maybe downright stupid and sometimes held out the hope that this person would change over time. Coupled with the assumption that two-parent families are more successful, produces the deficit model of being single parents. There is often a presumption of unmarried mothers especially the teenage ones.

What I know is that a lot of energy is put into judging those of us who floundered into less than useful relationships. There is also a perception that young black girls have babies to get a council flat and to get away from their parents.

The words that initially motivated me to move on came surprisingly from my mother, who one day in the 10th-floor tower block flat I shared with my then husband and three sons, said, "If the bed you made isn't comfortable, get up and make another one." This was said, of course in her Bajan accent, but the message was clear. And so, I did. With support from agencies, I moved to an old house in East Ham. It was one of those houses with a cross on the side. The cross did not indicate a religious belief but noted that these ancient houses had been pinned to keep upright and my boys and I were safe here. This went against the trend of 'you make your bed, you lie in it,' which I know was the view of many around me. Of course, I became the talk of the town (lots of people in our area knew each other from 'back home' and I can fully understand their view, but with my family behind me I got on with it.

Was it hard? – Hell, yes it was, but options become very limited when you have a little one to look after. Did I look unwell and unhealthy – yes, I did. Colloquially speaking, I spent much of that time being knackered, but somehow could put a brave face on. It is not hard to pinpoint where this strength came from, as I come from the separated generation where parents left children behind and came to England.

They would send for their children anywhere between 5 and ten years. I had, on reflection, developed some tools to deal with distress and trauma. I think I have always presented myself as being more confident than I felt.

In the tower block, I was not only looked after my children, but also the child of a friend and another relative.

On an ad hoc basis the occasional child who was too ill to attend day-care and their parents had to go to work, they would land in my care, life was chaotic.

I was bright and had passed my 11+ in Barbados, but coming to England at the age of 12 and ending up in a Secondary Modern school, I realised that (here was nothing modern about it!

I was met with the poor-quality education being provided for the sick working-class children, which meant that I pretty much drifted through the next few years.

When I left school, I took a six-month course and became a Comptometer Operator. This was a compromise, as my dad wanted his children to do better than him and wanted me to go to college, but we were a poor family and this course meant I still got a piece of paper and a good office job. With three young children later, I became a home machinist with a St Lucian lady called Kathy helping me.

It was Kathy who introduced me to a sewing factory, on Freemason Road She oh so kindly and forever etched in my memory, left her sewing and came to my flat to teach me how to sew. With a hired industrial machine (my mum hired it) I eventually learnt to sew fast enough to supplement my social security income by an amount agreed through this social agency. In the process, I mangled several garments, as I struggled to translate the many pieces of cut materials into the sample the factory delivered. I ran the needle through my fingers on many occasions, but that pain meant that I soon learnt to be extra careful. What Kathy's kindness enabled me to do was stay at home with my boys. However, back in the day, making a skirt was 10 pence, a dress 20 pence and a lined dressing gown about 30 pence (it was the 70's). Therefore, from 5a.m. to 10p.m. I sewed, while looking after the children.

Dealing with children with a range of medical conditions – grand mal epilepsy, asthma, broken limbs and the usual childhood conditions, meant that I became efficient and pragmatic and got on with it. I am still not sure how I got my eldest son to Hackney children hospital for regular check-ups on his epilepsy, while also having the other two.

Grand Mal seizures are unpredictable and, apart from the spectacular convulsions, the period of confusion that follows can last up to 48 hours. Also getting three children ready to take and collect from day-care was not even on the radar.

Much of what went on is a blur, but between my three sons, they can recall much more than I can – years on autopilot does that to the memory I think. The way I sum up those eight years was living on autopilot – doing what had to be done. No great highs, no significant lows and on at least two Saturday nights a month, I went off to All Nations club or a party somewhere, with my friends, while my parents looked after the boys.

At my 10th floor flat I had regular visitors, mostly other young mums, family and a few with nowhere to go/live – they kept me company throughout the day and most evenings. This gave me space to have a chat while sewing. They also got a meal of mostly mince, corn beef or beef brisket, lamb neck with rice and vegetables – in fact, the cheapest meals possible, but then we were all in pretty much the same boat. My mum, who regularly fed unannounced visitors at her home, always said, "If the food you cook can feed two people, it can feed three." So, these were pretty good days, as none of us fully understood the situations we were in. We just were!

FAMILY

Was I a single parent? I always give credit to my family for playing a significant role in bringing up my children.

My sister and brothers offered financial support once they started working.

One brother got them engaged in cricket so that their weekends were focused on positive experiences and when my other brother could afford a car, he collected the boys to take them to my mum and dad at the weekend. This meant I could get on with my sewing. My parents, however, were the stars in this process. They, without any overt judgement, helped bring up their grandchildren – provided food and pocket money, as well as visited regularly. When I moved to a house, my dad planted vegetables in the garden every year. This powerful force meant that I could hold my head above water and keep moving forward.

MOVING FORWARD

After about six years my life took a very positive turn, and I began to see the light most unexpectedly. Still pretty much in some fog, several events occurred. East London Black Women (ELBWO) started up, The Sickle Cell Society started up and I was invited to be part of the setting up of these groups, and two years later I started an Access Course at City and East London College, which culminated in me moving onto North London Polytechnic and gaining a Bachelor of Education (Honours), which started my career in teaching. I immediately undertook my Master of Arts in Education. Many of the women in ELBWO were also surfacing from challenges, and the mutual encouragement meant that many of us decided to go back to studying. The Sickle Cell Society gave me the tools to visit sufferers in hospital and talk to doctors and nurses at a time when little was known about the condition. I also had the opportunity to visit families at home, offering them support in getting better services. Setting up the first branch of the Society in East London meant that I learnt a lot about applying for funding.

I also was competent by this time with employing staff to research the number of families, their needs and services and culminated in a Sickle Cell/Thalassemia counsellor being appointed, after much negotiation with the local health authority. When the local African/Caribbean groups got together, we acquired funding to build a centre. At some point amidst all this, still looking after three sons, I became Chair of the local Race Equal organisation. I became a governor (including a spell as Chairperson) at my sons' secondary school. My boys rubbed alongside me. When I started my degree, they were at primary school and by the time I graduated they were all at secondary, so the need for me to be on hand before and after school and during the school holidays had passed. I also worked in a children's home during the long holidays while studying. The question is really when do you become just a woman with children abandoning the label of a single mum? The term 'single mum' was not part of our narrative when we were going through our experiences. I was just one of several young women bringing up our children with absent fathers, although the terminology 'absent fathers' was not in mainstream everyday language If it was in the sociology and psychology books, then those of us it impacted on were not aware of such terms. Some men kept in close touch with their children, and some didn't. We got on, the best we could, with the situations we found ourselves in. My children last saw their father when they when the eldest was five years old, and at some point in their twenties decided a joint visit was needed. Not a particularly successful encounter from their feedback. I do think that much credit has to be given to these young children who were faced with having to watch one parent struggle to bring them up, too young to appreciate that other parents and I were finding our feet and learning to knock down/overcome stereotypes and other multitudes of barriers. I accept that some were not able to do this. Having to work and bring up children on your means something has to give, and often what suffered was time, quality or otherwise, as the parent had to focus on financially supporting their children. This is not only the case for 'lone' mums.

The notion of being confident held out during this new phase in my life as I became Chairperson, Secretary or Treasurer in any number of groups and also represented the Caribbean Centre on two council committees. This new pattern carried on in Education and eight years after joining the profession I became a head teacher and had been leading schools for 24 years. In my early years of teaching, I realised that the skills and experiences I had acquired from my community/ voluntary work were transferrable, giving me a level of confidence, at the time still 'acting as if' to apply for my first promotion in my second year of teaching. I soon became aware of the progression ladder in education and with encouragement from colleagues, and friends, grabbed every opportunity to progress up the ladder.

FAQs – *how did you do it? When are you going to write your book?*

What must not be underestimated is the emotional toll on my wellbeing. Remaining as upbeat as much as possible would suggest that it was all-effortless for me. What was possible was being able to detach and carry on regardless. Regardless of what was being said, irrespective of the level of tiredness that can sometimes get right into our souls. Regardless of the scary moments, regardless of hanging on by my fingertips in the early days of studying when a whole new world of academia opened up and the fog returned while I figured out how and what to study. My lasting memory was a comment by a tutor in my first year of studying which said: "this sentence is out of control!" I thought it was a jolly good sentence myself and in what way it was out of control, she did not specify, and as in learning to sew, bit-by-bit clarity came. What also happened was a new 'family' of friends, and we were all in the same boat. In the primary, young parents who were on this new journey of discovery, in a culture that had low or no expectation of our community. We challenged openly and when a strange experience of being called to a meeting and asked why the Black students were not integrating with the White students, we were able to challenge why it was our responsibility to mingle and why were the White students not being asked the same question. However, the opportunity to study was a critical part of coming out of the fog and the four years at North London Polytechnic was indeed some of the best of my life at the time. Lots of new learning. No student loans back then. All students were given the grant to study.

ROLE MODEL – BUILDING LEGACIES

I am saying yes – when not sure what I'm saying yes to.

One day I had a call at school from a colleague at the Teachers' Centre (1989 I think). She had acquired some funding to provide Assertiveness Training for Trainers. The plan was that once the twelve chosen trainees had completed the programme, we would then provide assertiveness training for other teachers. Assertiveness at the time was an American concept, which had not yet crossed the water, and it from there that a super-confident trainer came. I did not have a clue what assertiveness was, but I said yes, of course, I would be interested. What followed was that for several years after, one of the local colleges funded Assertive sessions at ELBWO and I ran at least two 12 weeks (7 pm to 9 pm) sessions each year until the building was, sadly, burned down around 1997. What I learnt from this 'passing on' and is that my confidence began to develop, as I had to practice what I preached. During this period I went from 'acting as if.' to 'being' for most of the time, but this is still a work in progress. It's essential to take on opportunities while working towards being confident and not wait to be convinced before stepping into the uncomfortable and the unknown. Confidence is not an event but a process.

As a Black leader in Education, I have had the opportunity to step into the unknown and learn and equally importantly, to share. It is possible to work within the educational field and have an influence on the thinking and actions of the practitioners. Being within the school system and allowed me to have both power and experiencing the impact of being at the forefront of raising aspirations and expectations of children who find themselves in 'disadvantaged areas' and that the disadvantage does not lie within the children and therefore they can chart their journey. Of course, that has involved convincing adults that this is possible and also involved hanging onto the dreams for young children as we often forget that we cannot put 'old heads on young shoulders.' I have also had the opportunity to be part of teams who have worked tirelessly to change the face of leadership in education through developing and leading programmes, with ongoing support for potential and current BME leaders. We, who have spent much time stumbling through life, must not now take the high ground and damn young people. I have grabbed the opportunity to speak at conferences, run workshops, design my training materials and work with a range of organisations. I am particularly proud of my work in enabling others to chart their path through this prickly journey called life. To date I have coached and mentored more people than I can recall and as I begin to plan my exit from Headship am designing my business plan to support the strengthening of the leadership team, preparing potential/new leaders for the influential role of leading schools, and mentoring and coaching and reflect in wonder. As my skills from volunteering within the community translated into my teaching career, so too these skills and expertise honed in the field provide the bedrock for my new venture.

WHO AM I?

Alongside the community work of the late 70s and 80s, I set out to learn about my history and myself. I attended weekend courses on self-development. I recall sitting on the floor on one particular Saturday, holding hands and facing another participant and the task was around seeing within and saying what we saw and felt regarding the soul and spirituality of the other person. Clueless. Didn't quite know what I should be feeling. I attended many such sessions back in the day. A twelve-week (Sundays) programme on African History, which did not start with slavery, was a crucial part of my enlightenment. This was organised by the London branch of the New Jewel Movement – before the traumatic events that took place in Grenada in 1983. Angela Davis, Alice Walker, Terry McMillan et al., Ellen Kuzwayo "Call Me Woman" and her experiences of living in South Africa, matched by Bell Hooks 'Ain't a Woman?' All helped to shape my growing awareness of injustice and formed part of my journey to enlightenment. Many books on Emotional Intelligence, confidence building, assertiveness and spiritual awareness became part of my regular reading diet. Some autobiographies have been extremely useful as part of my learning and in response to the question. "When are you going to write your book?" I reply that somewhere in the many autobiographies that have been written over the years is my story. I still occasionally buy such books, but I have so many that I don't need to. Some people buy shoes, and I buy motivational books. I have a few I go back to again and again. Old favourites - It only takes a minute to change your life! By Willie Jolley. In the Meantime by Ilyanla Vanzant, Feel the Fear but do it Anyway – Susan Jeffers, I am Going on a Bear Hunt by Michael Rosen (a children's storybook with a message of bravery) and equally importantly other single parents, friends and inspirational people I have met over the years whose stories of going through and overcoming take my breath away, and I ask the question that is usually asked of me – "how did you do that?"

I do think that is defined as a single parent has been superseded by new labels, however the experience has come in handed over the years and I have pulled it out of the bottom drawer on occasions such as when challenging low expectations of children, when working with parents who suggest that I would not understand their challenges (from what they perceive to be my lofty heights of headship) and who would have imagined that living on the 10th floor of a tower block in Canning Town in the 1970s would have a part to play when helping others.

KEY LEARNING

Reflection and hindsight

Having the language of thought means that I can look back, in a rational, clinically way, and acknowledge my part in my life journey so far. What I have learnt is any decision I have made has been based on what I knew at that time, and that's the best any of us can do. Sometimes negative results, sometimes positive. "You cannot put old heads on young shoulders" is worth remembering when we are quick to criticise young people. Yes, I should have known, but I didn't. And if any of us are operating today as we did 20, 30 or forty years ago, we have not grown and can remain quite intolerant of others. And for many single parents, the right relationship comes along, and the best we can do is to learn not to live on alert all the time and remain open to embracing new opportunities.

My three sons are now in their 40s, and all are carrying on the legacy of 'family' and answering the call to action – which we must all do, in our way. I am now a grandmother.

Marva Rollins OBE

ABOUT ANDREEN CEPHAS

Andreen Cephas is an accomplished, highly experienced Cosmetologist, Trichologist Artistic Director of Hair Extreme Beauty and Barber Concept, Instructor, Trichologist External Verifier locally for City and Guilds International, Curriculum Writer, First Vice President to the National Association of Hair Dressers and Cosmetologists locally.

Born to Lolita and Ivan Rose, Andreen Rose-Cephas is the last of nine siblings known. She is a Philomath for education. Andreen's motto is that whatever your mind conceives you can achieve. This is a proven fact since she possesses certifications from some of the most prestigious institutions in the Technical Vocational.

These are fulfilled across three continents: Europe, The Americas and within her Caribbean region.

With proven recommendations in her field as Expert Judge at word skill Jamaica, Curriculum Writer, and a local External Verifier to City and Guilds International, Andreen Cephas has added to her many accolades.

In a field so highly, competitive she keeps pushing ahead as an industry leader.

August 2018

ANDREEN CEPHAS STORY

STILL I RISE

Life has its share of disappointments, or so they say. I was awarded a blessing at the tender age of 17, a teenager still in high school with a bright future. This was a time when most girls wanted makeup, jewelry, and fancy clothing. For me, it was a setback. The summer holidays in 1987 would have meant me returning to school, but it was short-lived.

The Christmas term approached, and the celebrations were in high gear, after all, it was Christmas. My sisters thought I looked unusual and told my mom, but the truth came in a glass filled with red label wine, a favourite to most Jamaican family back then. This would confirm their suspicion. The alcohol content had me vomiting all over the place. This caused concern, and I was whisked away to the clinic the next day, Monday. Their worst nightmare was confirmed, and my mother fainted under the June plum tree after receiving the news.

Life changed; I was moved from being the sweet baby sister to the disgrace of the family. The inner city I lived in at the time made my life a living hell. I got teased; at one point I was told I swallowed the netball. I was placed in the Woman Centre, a place for teenage mothers to continue their education and be put back in high school. My bundle of Joy came April 24, 1988, weighing 7 lbs., 14 ounces.

Throughout the pregnancy, I got little support from the father, but his sisters helped whenever they could. I was placed at St Andrew High for Girls after Mark was born. The minimal support continued, but this would not happen without sexual favours being given. I couldn't continue; I felt used and I could not afford to disappoint my parents again. Teenage motherhood was not something to proud of, but I was never ashamed. I used disappointment as an appointment for something else, during my tenure at St Andrew. With the girls I encountered, I passed the knowledge I had about becoming a teenager and single mother and how difficult and heart wrenching it was.

Life for me was complicated since I had to juggle high school and motherhood. My dad, Ivan O Adolphus Rose, may his soul rest in peace, was a dad and a whole lot more; he was my saviour. He would babysit while I was at school since my mom was away working. He played both roles. The journey continued, juggling school and single motherhood, what should have been for one had to split in two. After two of the most challenging years of my life, graduation came in July 1990; I made my mom proud when she saw me graduate. The father, or should I say sperm donor, left for the United States of America, and that was it, the move from sometimes support to no time support was now present.

I was jobless and a single mother. I wanted more. My sisters would normally braid at home, and I learnt while assisting them, that they had migrated, and I decided that I would have to do something, so I started braiding and doing cornrows at home. I did this for almost two years. A great sportswoman throughout high school, I was awarded a sports scholarship to Excelsior Community College, where the intention was to revisit a few subjects and then continue to do business administration. The first year had me focusing on just that, until I saw the cosmetologist, and realized this would be better for me achieving the dream I had for my blessing, Mark.

After college, I worked at Black Beauty Salon, owned and operated by Mrs P Thompson, who gave me my first break. This allowed me a bit of independence as I was now able to contribute to my son's well-being and not be dependent on friends and family. Miss Carol Sutherland, a friend to my older siblings, was employed at the transport authority and got me a temporary job. During the licensing process for the bus drivers and conductors, I became even more motivated. I was doing what others weren't in my community. I was employed. I did the unthinkable, got pregnant and beat the odds. I went back to school and was now working in an office. My motivation level skyrocketed. I was now able to feed and school my son well, or at least comfortably, or so I thought.

Being a single mother was and still is very hard. You never win, and there is always a missing link. This job was again short-lived, but I had to make the best use of it. I was made redundant after ten months and had plans to rent a chair in a salon to start my own business. That I did, but this meant long hours. Mark was now in preschool, and that cost me, but I denied myself to made sure he was ok. Primary school was next, and that meant more books, more money and more time.

With no help from the father, I was a lone ranger and would not give up no matter the cost. In September 1994, my son Mark was officially a 1st Grader. God had kept us this far, this was proof we had passed the worst. One of the hardest things as a single mother is not having the answers to why I am the only parent; I kept it positive and never told him a bad story about his dad. That had to be his decision. As the years went by, he grew and so did the bills. Life became more and more difficult. The chair I rented to start the business was close to my community, but things had gotten slow, so I had to think fast. I started hunting for a new space, and that's when I went, UPTOWN. Hours now turned into days not seeing my son awake, since I worked late almost every day.

Being self- employed and a single mother was even more difficult, and the difficulty comes when you can't fill the gap of the other parent. I never mastered it, having tried every method to ensure my son got the best parenting I could offer with the guidance and help of my mom and dad.

1995 and 1997 were bitter years. My sons' closest cousin migrated, and we lost my Dad in 1997. Everything I had was gone, and it got more complicated with Mark. He didn't cope well with the loss, and he stopped eating and became rebellious. I was in a corner not knowing what to do, but I had questions and got referrals where to get counselling help for him. High school came and went, struggles got harder, but my strength and will power got stronger. I was and still am destined to win and master single motherhood; after all, he is all I had to call my own.

September 1998 was another setback. I lost my Grandpa and also the space I was now operating from. I was asked to leave because I was not allowing my clients to be done by someone else in the salon. With little saved since the profit margin was small, I was living hand to mouth. Days went by, and I didn't eat, and if I did it was just one meal. I denied myself continually, so Mark was ok. I was broken. I had to work, and Mark had to eat and go to school. My friend Owen, a barber in the salon I was at before, introduced me to a new beginning, at least so I thought. This turned out to be a disaster. It lasted three months, and then catastrophe struck again. The bathroom clogged up and was spitting everything on the floor; I had to make a quick exit. Sadly, I had to return home.

Life became more and more difficult; I cried at night when my son was asleep, and it's not that my mom wasn't there because she was, and she did her best. I just felt this should be my responsibility. My mom was the best Grandma ever. I was allowed to do a few hairs on the Veranda, but they weren't enough to take care of my bills. More often than not I had nothing.

Andrea, my cousin, may her soul rest in peace, was many times my saviour. Andrea was my cousin by my dad's side. We were close. I met her in my teenage years and thanked God I did. She became my best friend since all my sisters had migrated and I was the only one in Jamaica. I never had anyone to turn to. My sisters helped as much as they could. Loneliness is a strong feeling, I lacked the sense of belonging, and at times I felt like I wasn't good enough, but Mark made sure I never forgot he loved me. Lolita (mama) kept me as best as she could; she was my physical shoulder to lean on. There were many times she was my only way out.

Hunger wreaked havoc in my stomach many times over and over between 1995 and 1999, and it was hard. There was a time I had one pair of jeans pants, so I had a dressmaker (seamstress) make me some shirts, and I would dress them up with scarves and anything else to make them look different. I saved a lot and undoubtedly that helped to start my new business. I had fifty thousand dollars in the Credit union, and I got a loan of 3 times that amount. That, along with a one thousand dollar investment from my sister, gave me enough money to start my salon, SHADES OF ESSENCE, now called HAIR EXTREME.

Mark struggled a lot with personal rejection although I tried to make him as happy as possible. In the summer of 2010 after returning from a vacation overseas, he was excited and said he wanted to continue to study abroad. He was enrolled in an Associate Degree at Crown Olympia Community College. He had taken the entrance examination at Howard Community college and passed. Sometimes life has a way of working itself out. I had asked one of my siblings probably three years prior if they could accommodate him overseas but that fell through. I could understand why they never thought I could finance his schooling. I had been saving for this time, and he went, all fees paid up.

Mark was doing well in his associate degree in architecture, and he even got a piece of his work on display in the Nature House. But he lacked motivation and focus, and he derailed. The conception of my first grandchild was now in play. I was devastated, not on becoming a grandmother, but for him not being ready. This cost him dearly, undoubtedly, but he took on his responsibilities, and he was the best dad he could be. I would have preferred for him to return home, but he differed and stayed to ensure his daughter had her dad.

He got married, but that did not last. In my estimation, they weren't ready, they had constant disagreements, and it was never resolved. He left and went to stay with his cousins, but he felt he had disappointed me and he was ashamed, filled with guilt of failure. I supported and encouraged him the best way I could. On May 6, 2013, I stood in the classroom at Heart College of Beauty Services and was getting ready to deliver the day's lesson. It was like any typical day, and it was quite unusual when I heard the phone signals of delivery of messages. I thought it was one of the students until I listened to a student bellow, "miss Ansa diphone", or "mi ago Ansa it fi yuh". I never take my phones to classes; I felt it was a distraction. However, this time they were there, and the messages were coming in at high speed.

I picked up both phones, and there were streams of messages. My gift wanted to give up, he no longer wanted to live. The good thing about having a close relationship with your children is that they will reach out to you even in their darkest hour. I froze. I could not think, I felt my heart pounding, I gasped, took a deep breath and asked to be excused; I stepped outside and looked up to my master and spoke to him.

I called my son on one phone, my sister was on the other line, I couldn't break. I had to be strong; my son on the other line had swallowed some pills. His speech was slurred and he was losing consciousness, so I had to keep talking. I got my sister Novelette, but she was too far away. Michell was closer, and so was Amanda his cousin. She was on her way back home, but when the Lord says move you have to move. Amanda had a stomach ache while on the bus to work, so she had to hurry back home - that was simply the Lord telling her your cousin needs you! I left the classroom and rushed to my vehicle that had to serve as my inner room. I had to speak to my master; I gave him thanks for giving me another chance at parenting and for keeping my gift safe, "I said Lord I know you can walk on the waters and fly over the sea so please get there before I do" and he did. The paramedics came, and god stepped in and my son was taken away to a sanatorium. I taught until 5 pm that evening. Then I went home, to continue to intercede with my lord. The family support was there but minimal, except for my mother. It's not that they didn't want to, but they didn't understand.

Depression was a tough cookie; it's a constant battle of self-doubt, sadness, sorrow, discouragement, disappointment… all of which he experienced. He never had that: at least not with me, except that his biological Dad rejected and lied to him regularly. Prayers worked every time, and God had him in his arms. That's a single mom's, as a matter of fact, all parent's nightmare.

My son was now struggling, and I had no support. Frankly people thought I was spoiling Mark. They didn't understand the intricacies of depression, and I had sleepiness nights like I was living on a time bomb. I tried everything to make him physically feel wanted. The burden was heavy; I carried it alone, just my lord and me. I would have support but didn't because my clients were my support. They listened, all the time. To date, my family still doesn't understand depression. One thing I know for sure is that he is a warrior for life. He got through that, yes he did; he fights every day to live.

Life became a struggle for me as well; daily I tried to celebrate life. I got very hard on myself; I felt I was a no-good mother. I thought I was to be blamed for sending him to school. Everyone was at me. I was now at fault for keeping his head up, so he could not drown. I fell into depression too, but I hid it. My husband started treating me like the scum of the earth. I was alone and afraid.

Helping my son caused a rift within my marriage, and there still is one. I can't deny or leave my son especially when he needs me. The challenges were many, but I took each one as they came, and I thought I did well. College came. I invested but there was no completion. But, I have not and will never give up. We all blossom at different times. If all blossoms were to blossom at once, the world would be a dull place to live.

Thirty years is a long time; enough to fill a whole book, but the long and short of it all is through it all – the struggles, the pains, the laughter, the tears – I would have done it again a little different, but again and again.

I am now the Grandmother of 3 amazingly beautiful grandchildren children: Maliha, Adjani, and Keonne, whom I love a world without end. Motherhood is a lovely thing, single or not, and we are so precious that we cannot be duplicated. Instead, we become continuums of parenting, with a prolific extension to our names. Through it all we are seen as the matriarch of the family whether the other parent is present or not.

KEY LEARNING

We have to take the good with the bad, take every disappointment and make it an appointment, every mess a message. Then continuously PUSH:

PRAY   UNTIL   SOMETHING   HAPPENS

If I may, I would love to attribute my complete success, motivation, tenacity, determination to my Mother, a woman who had kept me, even when I went down. She brought me back up and reminded me that there is a light at the end of every dark tunnel. It is her same strength I draw from hourly, daily and always remember all the insight she gave and still is giving. This Mom belongs to you.

KEY LEARNING

Our kids are kids no matter how old they are and we have to be there to support them regardless

I learned that you develop some serious resilience muscles as a single mother

That God has to be a huge part of the daily process

Andreen Rose – Cephas LCGI, Consultant Trichologist, Artistic Director Hair Extreme

ABOUT ANNETH BRYAN

Anneth Bryan (AKA Netty B) is the founder of Well Springs CIC and subsidiary NettyB.com. Anneth has over 15 years of work and training experience in social care, pastoral ministry and justice sectors, and has delivered over 5,000 hours of personal, lifestyle and business coaching. Anneth is regarded as being at the top of her game and is known as The Communications & Relationship Connector Expert.

Anneth took her childhood experiences of maternal mental health and enduring abuse and turned herself into a savvy, compassionate and innovative coach and entrepreneur with a portfolio business. Anneth utilises her unique skills and person-centred way of working to woo her clients while she shares elements of her personal story of high strength from tragedy to triumph.

Anneth received the call to pursue ministry and a career in the helping profession after experiencing personal and relational challenges in her teens, late twenties and early thirties.

Having experienced what she calls a 'Divine Intervention', Anneth somehow managed to find the strength and courage to overcome her difficult circumstances and continue in life. It is now one of her desires to help others who may be in a situation where they have run out of answers or who may need help to see the light at the end of their tunnel.

Anneth cites her two children Leon & Sherene as a source of inspiration, especially since the loss of their father in 2001. She attributes her strength through coping with her rekindled faith, her close-knit family. Anneth decided she would not allow the circumstances of their past life to stop her from having a future she deserved and as a result discovered that she had a passion for helping people and wanted to pursue this.

In 2006, Anneth enrolled at South London Christian College where she studied and completed Diplomas in Christian Counselling Psychology and Christian Ministry & Leadership. Anneth's professional, academic, ministerial and personal pursuits have run side by side, and an opportunity arose in 2007 for her to go to University to study Social Work.

Anneth realised that she needed to work out her purpose and refused to have any limitations on any future potential. She chose not to allow her past to dictate her future. She relied on her faith, which carried her through her daily life, studies and challenges. Anneth held onto the certainty that nothing was impossible to those who believed!

As a result, she is now a sought-after coach who works with people wanting to move from Limitation to Expectation, from Procrastination to Acceleration and from Stagnation to Production (LEAP) — helping people to move on after crime, harm, conflict or abuse in any setting.

Anneth's gems of teaching, training and coaching which shows people how to handle harm restoratively have won her belief in her field of expertise, and by using her bespoke methodology, her clients have been able to cope, recover and take back their power for good.

GET OUT AND GET OVER
HOW TO COPE AND RECOVER AFTER
TRAGEDY, TRIALS OR CONFLICT

THESE SHOES AREN'T MAGIC.

Have you ever tried on a pair of shoes that didn't quite fit because they were too big or too small? Perhaps you really liked them, so you compromised the fit and bought them anyway? You even persuaded yourself that they would be all right on the night if you stuff them or sit down for longer to avoid the pain.

Maybe you haven't had to sacrifice on comfort in a physical pair of shoes, but possibly you've made sacrifices in your personal or business life or made choices and decisions that have cost you dearly. Perhaps you didn't find out until it was too late and there was nothing you could do to get out quick enough. The truth is that there are no three clicks and you're off to Kansas Dorothy, or a quick word to beam you up Scottie, or you Captain Kirk. You have no choice but to deal with the situation, and you sadly realise what has happened to you is not a TV program or a fairy tale story, it's your life. You're stuck in a situation you did not see coming longer than you hoped, a bit like wearing a tight pair of shoes you struggle to get off your feet. You realise later that it wasn't worth the squeeze.

From the age of fifteen, I walked in shoes which had no magic powers like Dorothy's and ones that led me down a path that changed the trajectory of my life, caused me pain, gave me sores and scarred me for eighteen long years. I was presented with challenges and situations that I never dreamt would have been a part of my walk through this journey called life.

It was a lovely spring evening in April 1985, and I'm in a club knocking back Malibu and Coke with a couple of friends while enjoying the music. We are all underage but managed to sneak in because we look and act older than we are. I'm having the time of my life in my shiny high heels.

I notice one of the DJ's as he walks across the dance floor. He's tall and slender, our eyes meet, just the once. His friends call him General B, but his real name is Charlie. Later that evening, as I'm back home, easing off my shiny tight shoes and taking off my makeup, I hear a knock at the door and guess who turns up at the flat? Charlie! My friend had arranged this behind my back. I wasn't impressed at all. She let him in, and he sat in the front room on the sofa while I stepped down the stairs slowly and reluctantly, as my feet were sore. As I entered the room and sat down, he started pestering me with his smoky breath and overpowering voice; "C'mon Anneth, talk to me". "No, I don't want to, I'm not interested. I want to go to bed. I have a boyfriend anyway". I lied to try and get him off my back, but it didn't work. He kept on and on at me.

Eventually, he talked me down and 'IT' happened. I felt violated. 'IT' was horrible. Have you ever been in a position where you felt violated or scared to challenge something that you knew was wrong? No matter how many times you try to address it, the person doesn't listen or care.

WHO AM I

My parents were born and raised in Jamaica but migrated and settled in the UK in the early sixties. They were both hard working and devout Christians. I have two sisters, Jen older than me and Dawn younger, and we get on excellently. My mum suffered from post-natal depression following the birth of my sister Dawn, which developed into an ongoing mental health illness. Sadly, this resulted in her having to be admitted to hospital and sectioned on several occasions throughout our childhood. My father worked away a lot, which meant we spent a lot of time with relatives and church family.

My childhood had many ups and downs; some days I would attend school, other days I wouldn't. Most Jamaican parents were strict, and mine was no different. Nearly everything we asked for was 'No', so we just stopped asking. I remember growing up thinking "daddy doesn't love me, daddy never gets me anything or gives me cuddles. Why would anyone who was supposed to love me be like that?" Sadly, I never got to ask those questions.

Beatings were a regular occurrence in our house, and this happened for the silliest of things such as not making our bed or tidying our toys away. As a child, I was naturally mischievous and often blamed my sisters for things I had done. One day, we were playing with matches and a candle in the bedroom, and I ended up burning the carpet. My initial thought was "Oh boy! I'm in for it now when daddy gets home".

That evening, I heard my daddy humming that all too familiar tune. "Oh no, Dad's home"! At that moment I knew it was going to be all over for me. I braced myself for the worst. Sure enough, mum spilt the beans. She told my dad that one of us had started a fire and ruined the carpet. He immediately summoned my sisters and me and asked, "Who did it"? I was so nervous, I quickly responded. "Daddy it was her", pointing to my little sister Dawn. She looked at me in shock and disbelief, as she knew I was lying. I couldn't face another beating. I did feel the pain for her for a long time as I knew it was wrong to blame her. But dad was scary.

THE TEEN CHALLENGE

It's summer 1983, I'm thirteen, and I've just had my birthday. As a typical teenager, I had instantly become more curious asking lots of 'why questions', which seldom got answered. It was weird to me because my friends could play outside, go to school discos, have sleepovers, and even went on holidays. I was never allowed to do anything like that.

All my dad would ever say is "you ask too much question, be quiet, you chat too much", so eventually I stopped asking and I stopped speaking. It got so bad that one day while my aunt was visiting, she challenged my father's strict treatment towards us and said, "You children can't even cough without getting told off".

Two years later at fifteen, a newfound boldness came over me. It was like I just woke up one day and thought 'confidence', or maybe it was just rebellion. Well, the long and short of it, I started staying out late, hanging around with older people, drinking and smoking which resulted in me missing school and eventually being convinced to run away from home. Yes, I went AWOL. And not for a short time either and for about two years my parents thought I was dead. My dad came searching, the police began searching on the odd occasion, but I was never to be found. My shoes took me far away from safety.

VIRTUAL FRIENDS

On my travels, I met Sandra. Sandra was a large lady with short-cropped hair and a gold tooth. She became my new friend. For the first time, I felt a sense of belonging. The problem was, Sandra got me into all sorts of things which I thought were cool at the time, but really, they weren't cool at all. However, to me it felt different because no one had ever rewarded me or given me things like the way she did. I felt special, and I felt appreciated; I think I felt loved. All I ever seemed to receive at home was beatings, being told to be quiet or put down; I didn't feel love.

Shoplifting was a big trend back then, and Sandra made it seem fun. She pressured me subtly at first and then would demand that I do it. Sadly, in my naivety, I got caught several times which landed me in front of a judge, and I ended up on a care order and was forced to live in a care home. I wasn't happy about it and was trying to make a plan in my head of how I could get out because all I could think about was that my freedom had been stripped away again; it felt like I was back at home but worse because it was harder to run as it was staffed twenty-four seven. Little did I know, Sandra had groomed me into a life of petty crime? I thought she genuinely cared about me. I was wrong. Despite my behaviour, deep down I always had a moral compass, unfortunately, this time it had gone way off course. So here I am fifteen years old with a police record as long as your arm. Did I even care at the time? Of course not!

A few weeks after moving into the Children's home I started to miss the fun and freedom I enjoyed with Sandra. I wasn't settling, and I knew I wanted out, so I planned to run away. The evening came, the other children had all gone to bed and the night staff was nowhere to be seen. I had already packed a bag and hid it in my room with a few essentials. Time seemed to stand still that evening, but I was ready; it was time for execution. Eleven thirty PM and I made my escape out of the window while everyone was asleep. I'd saved the weekly pocket money, so I had enough for train fare and a taxi to Luton.

I had no idea what I was going to do when I got there, but that's where I was headed. I arranged to meet Claire, the woman who let me stay at her house before. The mad thing was I ended up getting into no good, and that's when I first met Charlie at the club.

MY BODY NOT YOURS

It's three months later after 'IT' happened. "I've missed my period again, Oh no! I don't know what to do"! I didn't say anything but knew I had to tell someone soon. All I could think about was that night after the club. I didn't want to do 'IT', and if it weren't for my so-called friend, I wouldn't be in this situation now. A few weeks later the police came looking and found me at Claire's. I was devastated because they swiftly escorted me back to the children's home. I was not happy.

So, you find me one evening laying on my bed thinking about my life. Barely sixteen and pregnant. "Oh God! What on earth have I got myself into? Is Daddy going to kill me"? I'm scared. The next day the social worker called a meeting to tell me the plan they had for me. They all thought that I was too young and too vulnerable to look after a baby and the only options given to me were abortion or adoption. "Adoption or Abortion", I repeated this in my head several times. "What! Who does she think she is"! I thought. "She can't tell me what to do, it's my body," my rebellious head roared. So, I contacted Charlie straight away and told him what she had said, and he told me to run away again, "just run, I'll look after you". He promised.

Have you ever felt like piggy in the middle? Well, that's exactly how I felt at that moment. "Who do I listen to? I can't go home, I'm worried, and I'm scared of telling dad". Being pregnant at my age made me feel like an outcast, and I felt like I'd humiliated my family, I couldn't face my dad, not in a million years. So, I decided to run in the opposite direction back to Charlie. After all, he had promised to look after me, whatever that meant.

Luckily, I was more resilient than most, and I found a bedsit as we needed somewhere to live. Sadly, it wasn't until we were together every day that his dual nature started to come out. He was nice as pie one day and the next day it was like living with a monster. I never imagined living with him would be like that. Even though I knew it didn't start right, I somehow falsely trusted him. What a mistake, as all he did from then on was control and abuse me just like Sandra did. I was too young and naive to notice what was happening and I couldn't say no. After some time, the police caught up with me, and yet again, escorted me back to the children's home. In one way I was happy to get away from the control and abuse, but in another way I was sad.

Three months later, I gave birth to a beautiful nine-pound baby boy, and I named him Leon, which means kingly, grandeur, and courage. Back then I needed bags of courage to face what lied ahead. Shortly after Leon's birth, I found the courage to visit my parents. Surprisingly they received me with open arms, and my mum said I'd given her the boy she never had, that was my invitation to come home.

So, I moved back in with my parents. Charlie sadly got himself into trouble and was locked up so wasn't around to see Leon. I had a second chance, I thought, to start all over and make amends with my family and start a new path with my new baby.

Having Leon softened my father. I saw a different side to him from what I experienced as a child; he was open and warm and fully embraced my baby. But somehow, I still feared him. About a year after being at my mum's, I was offered a flat in Luton by the council. Charlie was also back on the scene and wanted to come and live with us. I wasn't sure at first, but I thought well, he is his dad after all. He convinced me it was going to be all right and the right thing to do. I could see that my dad was not overly impressed, but he let me decide for myself.

At first, everything seemed OK. We were playing happy families, and things were ticking over steadily. Leon was growing, I was growing but so was Charlie's double-sided nature. He was drinking and smoking more; he started gambling and was not present as much as he had promised. Nor did he help with his son as I had hoped. This hurt me as I started to go insular again and I started to resent him. Then it started, the verbal, the emotional and the physical. It seemed like nothing at first, and I would brush it off as being because he drank, or he was high, and I medicated my pain by focusing my attention on my beautiful baby boy.

Here am I, a year later finding myself putting up with his behaviour yet again. But this time I had a child. What could I do with a baby now? I couldn't run like I used to. I had responsibility. This was the path I chose, and these were the shoes I had to wear. I was swiftly reminded of the saying my dad always said when I was younger and up to no good, "So you think you are a big woman now"! Did I?

At nineteen I fell pregnant again and nine months later gave birth to a baby girl I named Sherene. Sherene is my sweetness of life. A total blessing and delight for me, I thought to have a girl would turn Charlie's heart and change things between us, but I was wrong.

Picture this, I'm now twenty-one years old, with two children under five, and I'm living with their so-called dad, who I realise now doesn't have any intention of changing, he's nothing but an abusive partner. The thing is, I always held onto the hope that things might get better, but they never did. I was undoubtedly walking in the wrong shoes longer than I anticipated. I had no choice but to resolve myself to the fact that this was my life; this was going to be the norm.

After all, I am a parent now, and I have a responsibility, even in the chaos. I was big! I had to act big, also though I didn't feel big. Dad was right. These shoes hurt but I couldn't tell anyone. I smiled and got on with it regardless.

JACKAL AND HYDE COME OUT TO PLAY

Charlie's was a very likeable character, and he had many friends who looked up to him. I would wonder why sometimes because behind closed doors he was a real Jekyll and Hyde. He would be fine one minute and tearing my head off the next. I could never quite understand why he was like this. I felt like a ping pong ball, and I didn't know where I stood from one day to the next. It was all becoming too much.

Despite this, over the next few years, I tried hard to hold things together for the kid's sake. I longed for days when he would go away so that I could have a little bit of normality, but that picture of 'normal' was far from my reach. What was normal? Did I even know anymore?

One evening after he'd been on a drinking binge, we had an altercation. Things were so bad by now that I had made up my mind I was going to leave. So, I planned it and left while he was asleep. No bags, no nothing, I just upped and took the kids. The next day when he realised I wasn't there, he came looking for me, something he'd done countless times before. This time I was with his sisters, and I knew he'd be over as soon as he realised. I couldn't sleep, but at least it was somewhere to get away for a few hours. The next morning, we were at breakfast, and I heard a bang on the door, my heart sank as I knew it was him. I went into instant panic mode like I did countless times before. I heard his voice shouting at me through the letterbox begging me to come back.

"Why can't you just leave me alone?" I yelled'.

'If you don't come back, then I'm taking Sherene"! he shouted.

He was banging hard on the door repeatedly with his fist, and his sister had no choice but to open the door. I was so scared, I froze. I didn't know what he was going to do; she was scared too. How could I protect my kids from him were my only thought, but I was helpless. I didn't trust the police; they had not helped in the past. I felt trapped. Charlie rushed in and tried to drag Sherene from my arms; the sick child was like a raggedy doll; I didn't want her distressed any more than she was. As much as I was holding on to her for dear life, I had to let go. I reluctantly loosened my grip. Charlie took her from me, walked out and put her in the car. I stood still, unable to move my legs became like jelly. My heart is beating faster than ever; I'm broken and in tears. What am I supposed to do now?

"Why Charlie? Why are you doing this to me"? I manage to run out and shout after him, by now he's got Sherene in the car, and he turns his head before getting in the driver's seat, looks back at me with his wry smile and speeds off. "Come back! Come back!" I shout; he ignores me. He's gone.

"Oh my Lord, what am I going to do?" He's just kidnapped, my baby! I hold my head in my hands and cry.

So, I'm contemplating what to do. Do I call the police? Or do I go home? Toying for ages trying to work out what to do. All these thoughts are rushing through my mind. "I hope he doesn't hurt her. No, he wouldn't, that's his daughter, but I don't know? I don't want to go back! I'm torn, I feel ripped apart inside, and my heart hurts like hell. I should call the police. But if I do that, he will kill me for sure". My emotions are heavy; I don't know how to feel. He has Sherene. He has my baby. I have no choice. I feel so trapped emotionally, physically and in my head right now. "What can I do"?

So, I talk to his sister, and she reluctantly convinces me to go back for the kids' sake. She hated the way he treated me as much as I did, but she couldn't even talk to him, he wouldn't listen to anyone.

So, the next day I take the dreaded journey back home. Can I even call it that? It wasn't home; there was nothing homely about that house. I knew I was going to go back to a flimsy apology or a long day or night talking me down with the empty promises. In my heart, I didn't want to be there, but he would never take no for an answer. I knew the happy family's sequel I dreaded had restarted.

"Have you ever been in a place where you felt like you had limited options or no choice"? Well, that's precisely where I was right at that moment. I had no choice.

PLANNING FOR PURPOSE

It's ten years later, and time has moved on, and things aren't getting better but they're not getting worse. The only thing that could get worse than how I was living was to be dead, but even death seemed sweeter than the life I was living. Despite these negative thoughts, I begin to tell myself that it was time I started to think about me. But I knew that every attempt to do something to better myself, Charlie would sabotage. I knew he didn't want me to break free, and he got jealous of anyone who tried to help me and quickly shut off the relationship. I really couldn't understand why. I always thought if he didn't want me, why wouldn't he let me go? So, I attempted to go to night school, but that failed, as he would always relent on his promises to have the children.

I hated the way he treated me but what was I to do? I felt like I had no power or hope left. I felt completely stuck. All I heard ringing in my head daily was "No voice, no choice". It felt like the rest of my life was doomed. "This is how it is, and this is how it's always going to be". These were regular thoughts that entered my mind. I tried so hard to fight them, and I would speak out loud, "Anneth you're strong. Anneth, weeping may endure for a night, but joy will come in the morning. Anneth, God will never give you more than you can bear." I would recite scripture after scripture, I would speak to God, I would tell God off, I would cry out loud, I would shout and bellow when on my own, and the anguish of my situation was too much to bear. I was so young and so stuck. Even though God's word promised that he would never leave me nor forsake me. I often felt abandoned by God in the early days and by my dad because I knew that I couldn't tell him how bad things were. I didn't have faith to believe that he would rescue me because I knew what he would say, and I was too embarrassed to put myself there as a 'big woman now'.

I had one hope and one hope only and that was to revert to relying on God, despite my unbelief. It worked for my mum so why not for me? I would often challenge God because we were always taught to walk by faith and not by sight but when you're amid what seems like a lion's den, how can you be so faith-filled? It was damn hard because all I was seeing was a living hell. I would often say, "If you're so big God and such a present help, then help me! Help me now! Help me get me out of here". I sobbed so often, night after night, I couldn't understand why God would leave me to suffer at the hands of a man for so long. I didn't get it, and I didn't understand.

I blamed myself of course because my dad always told me to watch it as a child, what did he mean? Was it because I didn't listen? Was it all my fault? What was I to wait?

I even began to believe I deserved to be treated this way because I was terrible as a child. After all, that's how dad made me feel. What on earth am I thinking?

Have you ever been in a place where you felt like there was no hope, or like there was no light at the end of the tunnel? Maybe there are times when you felt like giving up too because you thought what's the point in digging to try to get out because you can't see the light either. Or possibly you also have lost all hope. You have lost all strength to carry on.

I regularly visited this dark place when it came to Charlie. But somehow there was always a slither of hope inside of me, a little bit of strength would still rise in me even in the darkest of times when I thought I would never get up after a blow or I felt like this time he was going to kill. My body was active on the outside, but my spirit was weak on the inside. I was tired, drained, mentally and emotionally exhausted. God, are you there? Is God hearing me? Please hear my cry, oh Lord. Please answer my prayers.

SURFING FOR SOMETHING NEW

Charlie's moods always dictated my day, how things would turn out and even where I slept. He would often kick me out of our bedroom as a punishment for not conforming to his requests the night before or after an argument he started and couldn't finish. As a result, I spent many a night in my daughter's room whenever he decided to stop talking to me. I didn't mind as it was the only time I felt I got a bit of peace in my head as I didn't have to speak to him or argue back.

He thought he was punishing me by ignoring me but in fact, over the year's I'd developed a thick skin and turned it around. It was a blessing in disguise as I didn't have to put up with the emotional and verbal attacks. I'd learned to handle the cold shoulder and blatant ignorance. In the early days, I would look for affirmation but as I got older that changed.

It is September 1998. I'm at home in Sherene's room on the computer. Sherene's apartment was very peaceful, and quite frankly somewhere, I would often resort to for sanctuary when things got too much. Having time out to escape my reality felt good. It enabled me to meet new friends online which is where I met Tracey.

Tracey was from Florida, and we met on AOL chat. She quickly became my virtual friend and go-to person; she supported me emotionally. I was able to share things with her that I'd never told anyone before; it just felt safe. Partly because I knew she would never meet Charlie and I thought that he would never find out I was talking to someone online. I liked talking to her because she encouraged me and lifted my spirits on the darker days. Tracey also was very frank and threw me some hard-hitting truths when I needed to hear them too.

"Anneth you know you deserve better"? she wrote. "I know I do". "You are too beautiful a soul to put up with all that crap; he doesn't know what he has got! Why don't you leave him? Why are you still putting up with his abuse after all these years"? "He doesn't love you or the kids".

"What is the hold he has over you? I don't understand". "I don't know Tracey; I'm just really scared" I replied. "I feel stuck and have been like this for a very long time. I so badly want to get out, but I don't know how. What shall I do? Please help me, Tracey".

"Anneth I want you to know that you have all the power within you to get out and to live your life for you and your children, but you need to make up your mind and no turning back truly. No looking back. Remember what happened to the woman who looked back in the Bible, she turned into a pillar of salt. Now you don't want that to happen to you, do you, for you to become extinct! Do it now before it's too late".

Tracey's continued words of chastisement and encouragement instilled dread and hope in me all at the same time. But I hope it was something that I had not felt in a very long time; I was so used to only feeling fear, being rejected and accepting ridicule as my daily bread.

After all, I wasn't getting any real answers from God! I don't think he even heard my prayers and tries to help some of the time.

I don't even know if I believed anymore because Charlie had pressed me down so much over the years that I had lost all my self-worth and my faith in God was weaker than ever. I mean where was God all those times in the past when I needed him? How come he wasn't answering me? I felt as though I was lost in the sea of forgetfulness. At that moment all I had was hope in the words of Tracey.

Tracey was right! The kids are getting older, and I'm getting older too. It's getting worse! It's getting harder to protect myself and them; I don't want to be SALT. Running away for good seemed like my only option. "Being mentally and emotionally bound by his control must finally come to an end?" I said to myself. "I've made up my mind; I've got to do this if not for me but the kids. There's no turning back now."

I soon realised after my online chat with Tracey that what I was missing on previous occasions was a proper exit strategy!

"Yes! That's it"! This time I didn't care if I ended up dead, but I knew I had to forge a plan to get out and get out quickly! If not for me but my kids. So, it began.

THE POWER EXCHANGE

It's four months later and I find myself arguing with Charlie again! Only this time I was ready, I was more determined and defiant than ever before, because I had spent the last few months secretly building myself up. I recited every kind of positive affirmation I could find and learnt more and more about abuse and how women like me struggled, but how the determined ones made it out. The internet became my best friend; I researched and found the help that I didn't know was out there. This time I was finally ready for this next argument. I said "No"! "No, more"! It came out like a squeal at first, but it came out!

Charlie turned around, looked at me and said, "What did you say?"

"No!" I said even louder than the first time. "I'm not doing this anymore! I'm not taking your abuse! I'm not going to be your Doormat anymore!"

A sheepish look came over him, even though I could tell he was raging internally.

He couldn't believe it; I knew what was coming next – SMACK! I dropped, but this time I didn't curl up or stay down, I stood up, looked straight back at him and said, "I'm strong, and I'm leaving you"!

He was shocked that I spoke out. I can only describe that moment as a 'power exchange'. For the very first time, I felt in control. Although my face was throbbing, and my head was banging, I felt good inside knowing that I hurt this time, not because of fear, but because I stood up to him. Was there a God after all? Is my faith being restored?

From then on, Charlie started to back down, and the word 'No' was in my loaded gun, which I fired at him many times after that. Eventually, his threats, physical abuse and control had lost their power over me. I just kept on reloading my gun. No! No! No! No! No! Until those words meant I wasn't scared of him anymore.

MAY DAY MAY DAY

Tracey's words she wrote to me that day not only stuck with me but hit me deep down. I started to see a glimmer of hope and a reason to fight on. I always knew what I wanted to do, but Charlie had never allowed me to develop myself. I was a slave in my own home. Charlie had stolen my best years, my womanhood, my dignity, my sexuality, my voice and my choice. Here I was, now thirty years old and seeking a way out.

Now you must be wondering how I got out. How am I still here to tell this story? Let's say there was a final ending that broke my heart, but in many ways, mended it. Charlie gave me back my freedom in a bittersweet way.

THE BEGINNING OF THE END

It is a sunny morning in May 2001. The sun is drawing in and out interchangeably the sky's turning grey than bright. As I breathe in the crisp fresh air, I'm experiencing a mix of emotions, and I'm trembling and don't quite know how I should be feeling. I'm standing outside the building just about to enter and as I look around there are people everywhere, I can hear birds chirping, as I listen up, I see the clouds moving at speed as if they are going somewhere. "I wish I were on a cloud myself; I'd rather be anywhere than where I'm stood right now", I say to myself.

"What's going on with me, get a grip, Anneth for God's sake! Isn't this what you have always wanted"? There goes that voice in my head again. I'm struggling but at the same time trying to make sense of it all and I'm failing to understand how I am even here.

I step into the building, which at first sniff smells old and damp. As I walk further to the front, I look up at the high ceilings and around at the narrow lancet-shaped windows aligning every wall. I whisper to myself, "Oh God", but it comes out like a big echo, Oh God, Oh God because the ceiling isn't just high it's hollow too. Suddenly, this eerie feeling comes over me, and I can feel myself shivering all over from the inside out.

There he is in front of me! "Gosh you don't look the same, you're thinner, you have no colour in your face. It must be because it's cold in here I guess, you haven't even had a haircut, and it's still as thick I see, and that smirk looks as if it is permanently fixed to your face. No change there then."

As usual, I'm feeling unnerved by his presence but this time for a different reason. I look around, I see lots of people, some sitting, some standing and everyone's just looking my way. "Wow, he is a popular guy isn't he"? I'm feeling a little uncomfortable because everyone's crying and I'm not. Should I be? I don't know! I don't care, what they know.

I feel for my jacket pocket and take out the old crumpled photograph of me and the letter, in I breathe as I step towards him. Right, I suppose I'd better tell you now.

"Charlie I've written you this letter because I thought I would never be able to tell you face to face how I feel because I've always been too scared of you. I don't know if you are even listening to me, but I need to get this off my chest! I know I'm looking at this photo, but I don't recognise me. I look a bit different there". I look around and wonder if all these people knew about this if they would think a different way about you too? *This is the night after you went into a rage and you hit me, again. Look at all the bruises, look at my unrecognizable face! You did this not once but many times over the years". "I can hear and see everyone crying; but only my close friends know what you are really like".*

"You see the thing is Charlie, there are always two sides to every story and now I finally get the chance to tell you mine, and my side of the story is that for the last 18 years you have been an abusive partner. Eighteen long years I've been with you and look where we are today"!

"Yes, we had some good times but to be honest there were probably more bad times than good". "I didn't choose to be with you, you stole me remember". "I never expected in a million years that I would end up here, but I was just too scared to leave you".

"One day I was going to ask you why you did this to me, why didn't you just leave"! "And now that day is never going to happen and I'm sorry

your dead, but I'm not, as now I'm finally free". As I take another brave step forward, I lay the crumpled photo and letter in the coffin. *"Look after the old me won't you, goodbye Anneth, goodbye Charlie".*

I don't know if you have ever had a time when something's happened, and it's terrible, but you feel free at the same time? Here's the thing you didn't know. Charlie took his own life, and I was finally able to take off those shoes that for many years caused me so much pain and agony. From that moment forward I vowed never to try to fit into shoes that were too big or too small ever again.

JOURNEY THROUGH COPING AND RECOVERING

My life story of early childhood trauma and subsequent abuse may not be dissimilar to others you might have heard or read about. However, when you feel and see the effect of what going through something like this can have not only on the victim but also on children, family and friends, it's hard to contemplate how or why anyone would put up with this type of behaviour for such a long time.

My life with Charlie did something to me as a young girl and as a woman which I don't have enough pages to describe here. My experience did, however, make me realise I never wanted myself or my children to experience or feel anything like this again. So, I made a vow to myself that my future must be better than my past. That I was going to pursue my destiny and make up for all the years that were stolen from me.

My only option moving forward then was to be strong for them and me. It wasn't easy. I messed up,

I did. I even let them down at times, but we made it through also, though the odds were often stacked against us.

How did I cope? I coped by throwing myself into personal development. Admittedly I had a few meaningless relationships along the way; it was strange as I had been so used to living with the chaos that I didn't recognise or know what it was like to have peace and normality. Eventually, my moral compass kicked in, and I was back on course, and with encouragement from my daughter, I ultimately rekindled my faith in God, to the point where my faith became the basis for reshaping my whole world.

I was slowly but surely healing, through reading those same scriptures that I had lost all hope in years past. But for some reason, they finally made sense to me the day I needed them too. The day I made up my mind enough was enough.

God said he would never leave me nor forsake me. He didn't, nor would he give me more than I could bear. He didn't. I am still alive today to tell the tale. Was my tolerance so high that God pushed it to the extreme with Charlie? Was this all a test? Along with the exam I was destined to fail, or was this a pass that I could now use as a compassion compass to shape the rest of my life in helping others to avoid what I had experienced?

I was heading towards a new life I knew nothing about, but I was slowly beginning to find my feet. I eventually secured a new job which was more aligned to my purpose. I finally began to discover who I really was and gradually started to believe in me again.

My confidence grew slowly, and for the first time in my life I had goals; goals that I could see were achievable as nothing was stopping me now but for me. I went to college and also graduated from university. I tried my best to support my two children, not only to deal with the trauma of what happened to their dad but to try and rebuild their lives without their father. It was hard, because on the one hand, it was unfortunate for them but happy for me. I was caught in an emotional rollercoaster. I had to learn how to manage and separate my emotions quickly. After Charlie's funeral, I vowed to myself that I would never be so vulnerable again or let anyone control me the way he did. Today

I can honestly say my life is now my own, to live it the way I want to live it and how God designed it to be. I increased my faith, and I changed my mind-set, I finally accepted me. I am a different person now. I am no longer Anneth I am now Netty. I am no longer weak; I am strong. I am no longer fearful; I am fearless and ready to tackle the rest of my life.

Coming out and coming through a very toxic, abusive, controlling relationship, fuelled my passion and mission to learn about mental health, trauma and spirituality as I wanted to understand Charlie and my mum and my parenting. As a result of my knowledge, people naturally started to want to hear from me and I began informally counselling many individuals. Clients wanted me to share the strategies that I had used to cope, recover and move on.

Having also experienced a lack of bonding and attachment to my father as a child and the impact of my mother's mental ill-health, I realised these were some of the key drivers that led me into a life I had no business experiencing or why I made some bad choices. However, I don't blame my past or my parents. I choose to use my experiences as a stepping-stone now to push me towards my future goals.

My mission now, through my Personal Power Master Classes and my Destiny Builders Boot camp, is to help others build confidence, become more self-aware, resilient and educated to take back their power so that they too can live and love their lives and make the rest of their lives the best of their life. You might want to take this thought away with you: No one should ever wear a pair of shoes that don't fit them.

KEY LEARNING

NETTY'S TOP TIPS

Here are seven nuggets I'd like to leave you with that helped me in my life's journey and that I share with my clients.

1. Faith is essential, and it keeps you grounded when all else around you seems chaotic and out of control.

2. Take a peripheral view of your life at times: if you were to advise yourself on your current state what would that advice look like? Then take that action; this is the first step to healing yourself.

3. Remember we all have a purpose. It's up to us whether we fulfill it or not. Aim to see what that truly is, as life is for living not just existing. There is no cut and action replay.

4. We all get hurt at one point or another in life. Our job is not to stay stuck in that place but to use the experience as a learning curve to influence future choices and decisions more positively.

5. Don't ever beat yourself up over mishaps or misunderstandings, and it's OK, we all make mistakes.

6. If you are feeling sad or low don't fake it by saying 'I'm fine'. It's better to say I'm having a bad day, but I'm sure I'll get over it soon.

7. Forget or limit your time with toxic people even if a family member. If they're not for you, don't waste any more time trying to convince them to get them on the side.

As a reader of this book, you are entitled to a free 30-minute DISCOVERY consultation. You can email your contact details to info@nettyb.com to claim it.

ABOUT MARY WANJIKU

Mary Wanjiku is Kenyan born, a single mother of two sons and a daughter. She is the author of a Woman's World and the Men-In-between with the view of strengthening and empowering girls and women to fight their battles. She has a passion for working with families and children with special needs. She has volunteered in children's services, such as Sure Start, gaining a certificate of recognition for her services and Home-Start. She also supports new mothers at a clinic.

Mary's primary concern has been one of empowering women, especially those prejudiced by the systems because of their single motherhood status.

As a young mother, she was determined to provide for her child as her grandmother taught her the benefits of being independent. From school, her first job was a hairdresser and then she worked with a non-governmental organization supporting children and families living in poverty as an untrained social worker. She moved to the UK to study child development before going back to her NGO job, and she worked in special needs schools before starting a hair salon business, a café, and property development.

However, all these came tumbling down when her first relationship becomes sour. She gave her café to a relative whose husband left her with six children, and El Nino rains destroyed some of her properties, and she gave the rest to a relative.

A degree in social work in England enhanced her desire to help those who had no voice. One single mother once said at a child protection meeting "before working with Mary I was made to feel I had no right to speak by the professionals and Mary gave me the confidence to speak out". Mary believes that the rights of mothers and support are crucial in safeguarding the welfare of the children.

I AM STILL STANDING

Being a mother is the hardest job in the world. Although it is emotionally draining, it is the most rewarding. As a lone parent, multitasking is a must. Providing love, emotional wellbeing, laughter and necessities become a priority. It can be challenging without support. I have faced challenges since moving to England over seventeen years ago. However, despite everything, children come first in every decision I make whether it is work or relationships.

While at the university from 2012, childcare was the primary concern. I had to catch six buses to and from the university to another town. I picked the children up from the child-minder late, and as soon as I got home, I kicked off my shoes and headed straight to the kitchen to cook. Moreover, I helped the children with their homework, reading, cleaned and did assignments after they went to bed.

Throughout university, sleep was like a luxury. However, positivity was the key. My thirteen-year-old daughter once said there is no need to worry about things that I am unable to resolve because they will work out someday. I used to worry about bills, but now I take things one at a time.

Before graduation in 2016, I had agency social work job opportunity, but I was too stressed to take it, and dissatisfied with the way the systems worked with some clients. The next interview I did, I missed the job because of childcare. The job involved early and late shifts as a team leader. Therefore, working around schools with an agency became an option with less money but proved to be more flexible. I later got a contract at a school.

However, when I thought I was putting my life in order, I was diagnosed with stage four lung and breast cancer in March 2018. Through this, I continued working until my condition got worse in May 2018 while I went through tests and waited for treatment. I was afraid of not having enough money to support my children.

Despite the diagnosis and worries, I maintained normality in the home even when feeling weak and lethargic. I knew the children have friends at school whose relatives have died of cancer, and they talk about it, and I know this may have played in their minds.

Therefore, discussing my condition with them was vital. The children say that regardless of the treatment side effects it will make me better. They are a great support system with encouraging words. And when I get words like "you are the best mum in the world" from my thirteen-year-old daughter, and when my sixteen-year-old son tells me I'll get through it, and I should say "God I haven't written an application to go to heaven yet", it warms my heart. Sometimes we bury ourselves in the rubbles of our issues and financial struggles and forget the little things that make us and others happy.

It was a hard time for my son as he was about to do his General Certificate of Secondary Education (GCSE). During this time, I had a cough that wouldn't go away, and it worried the children. I felt terrible that I couldn't help him with his revision as much as I wanted to and even missed parents' evening, and my daughter's ballet show.

On one occasion as I coughed my daughter took my temperature, she stared at me and said, "Oh my God mum you need to call the hospital your temperature is over 39 degrees". At that time, I was freezing, and I had asked my daughter to get me another blanket, but my son said I didn't need a blanket because my forehead looked sweaty. I rang the hospital and my first concern was who to leave the children with at 9 pm and my son had an exam the following day.

I rang a friend, but she wasn't in. While contemplating what to do next, she rang back and came to pick the children up and took them to her house with her family and dropped me at the hospital. Straight away I was hooked on intravenous antibiotics and also given a drip. All I thought about while lying on the hospital bed was the children and how I disrupted my friend's time. The children were texting me asking when I would be home, and I kept on telling them I didn't know.

At 1 am I was transferred to the cancer patients ward as the blood test results indicated I had neutropenia sepsis. I was at the hospital for a week. My children slept at my friend's house but decided to eat at home. Moreover, my older son had been in a motorbike accident and was admitted to the same hospital. I am lucky to have two friends who brought the children to the hospital to visit me. I wondered how they felt at the time. Recently my son told me he was very scared when he saw me at the hospital because I looked very ill and it made him lack sleep and not concentrate on his exams.

Life was not always like this. When I had my first son at the age of twenty with my childhood sweetheart who I was with for fourteen years, my family and his mother supported me with childcare when I started work, before I employed a house-helper. I had no financial struggles. Perhaps that's why friends in Kenya don't believe I struggle in the UK.

After high school, being independent was a priority. My partner and I supported each other, and when I got a job with a nongovernmental organization, I earned more. I helped him out financially when he started a business. We gave each other space and contributed to the household needs equally, and we were happy. However, the more money he got in his company, the more things started falling apart.

There were rumors of infidelity from a friend and his cousin, but he insisted my friend was jealous. However, two women rang at home asking for him. I knew as a businessperson he had to deal with all sorts of people, so I was always polite to the women when they phoned.

However, on one occasion, I was selling a plot of land, and someone called demonstrating interest. I arranged to meet up at the gates of Nairobi city hall. However, my intuition told me not to go alone. I asked two work colleagues to accompany me. I wondered how the person knew about it.

I was late leaving work on that day, so we didn't get to meet the man, but I spotted him disappear into the distance before we crossed the road as he had described what he was wearing.

On that night a woman called and said she was with my partner at her house and also when he had been away from home. I asked the woman to put him on the phone. Instead, she told me if I left, she would be married to him since I was planning to go, and I didn't want to get married or have another child. The woman said she had sent the man I was supposed to meet. I was in a daze. I didn't know who she was, but she seemed to know a lot about my family.

As soon as the woman was off the phone, I called my partner's mother in floods of tears wondering what this man could have done.

As I spoke to my partner's mother, my son's father stormed into the house. His mother and brother asked him about the woman. He denied ever knowing her. However, afterwards, he called a number and asked me to listen and confirm if it was the woman. After confirming, he argued with the woman, and the woman called him all sorts of names. That night I did not sleep. The woman kept on ringing the landline when my partner switched off his mobile phone. She told me I was a victim of circumstance.

It made me anxious because I had no idea who she was. I couldn't stop thinking of a woman at a school I worked in who was shot dead in cold blood outside the school gate, and two weeks later her husband brought their three-year-old daughter to school with a girlfriend which raised the teacher's eyebrows.

So, knowing this, I confronted my partner and asked him if he knew the grave danger he was putting me in with this woman. He swore he had nothing to do with her and that she followed him when he was out with friends.

I decided we should part ways and there was no turning back. That night he told me if I didn't see him and our son who was eleven years old the following day, I should check our car at a certain escarpment. It sent a shiver to my spine because I knew the spot was a death trap. I didn't go to work and instead accompanied him to our son's school. I feared what could have happened if I didn't go. He warned that he would never leave me. He said I was a lovely quiet girl when we first met, and I didn't love him because of money, but I had changed.

We parted ways when I moved to England, and I left with nothing. Despite me having another child, he still wanted us to be back together. But I was done with him. I lost everything we had built in the fourteen years we were together. He never supported our son, but we remained in touch.

I had separated from my second son's dad because of jealousy. If a man smiled or looked at me, there were accusations that the strangers were interested in me and this made the relationship toxic. I found it mentally draining. His insecurities were affecting our relationship.

I asked him to separate while in a car in London, and he went crazy and drove the car fast. I thought the car would crash. He wondered how I could ask him to separate when he loved me. I calmed him down and told him we could still be friends, but he didn't want us to be just friends.

At this point, I didn't even know I was pregnant. I did a pregnancy test with a pharmacist, and there it was. I was six weeks pregnant. I decided to take care of the baby alone. When I called him and told him about the pregnancy, he smirked and said I didn't want to be with him. He asked to be together, but I said no.

I moved to Derby, and he remained in London. We saw each other a few times, and he was there at birth. However, due to illness, we didn't get to register our son's birth certificate. He was helpful around the house, but after two weeks the jealousy emerged. I had gone to a corner shop near my house, and he had followed me without my knowledge. When I came out of the shop, he asked me why I was talking to the shopkeeper smiling. I stared at him, and I knew he would never change. I asked him to pack and leave because I couldn't stand nonsense.

We arranged to register the baby, but when he was on his way, he asked me to marry him, and I said no, and because of that he refused to come. He later got married, but before he got married, he asked me to marry him. He came with his wife to see our son when he was two years old, and that was the last time he saw him. After three months he told me he had separated from his wife and moved to Italy. I was not surprised.

There was no financial support, but we kept in touch. However, we lost contact when I forgot my handbag on the bus after visiting my daughter's father at the hospital with a broken leg. I was juggling the children, the pram, and some bags when this happened. However, a former neighbor said he had come looking for me, years later but I had moved to another area.

My handbag had about two hundred pounds, documents and my phone. My daughter was a few months old. Her father had convinced me to have a child together and accused his ex-partner of denying him to see their son despite him supporting her. I encouraged him to speak to her but later found out from her after he started seeing his son, he never helped her. And here I was no house keys, no money and no food. I tried ringing my phone, left messages begging for the documents and the keys to be thrown in my garden, but the phone went dead.

I felt stuck in a rut. Somebody advised me to go to a food bank. I had no choice. The bank gave me some money which I bought baby stuff. I found it hard to ask my daughter's father for money because we were not on good terms. However, I thought after knowing the situation he would have helped. I continued supporting him and taking him clean clothes at the hospital. And when he left the hospital, I fed him, cleaned his wounds and helped him get in the bath.

Once he recuperated, he asked if we could move to Kenya and get married there. I told him I wasn't ready. I didn't want to plunge into unknown territory on shaky grounds.

He told me he would sell his house for us to start a business. He had several trips to Kenya staying up to three weeks. But when he told me his suitcase was stolen from the London coach station when coming back from Kenya, my instincts told me something was fishy. When I questioned him, he seemed nervous.

After one of the trips, I discovered an email from a female and the woman was talking about buying a house with him and getting married in Kenya.

I confronted him about the email. He denied it at first before I showed him the email, and he went quiet. He apologized and said nothing was going on despite the email. He sent an email to the woman and told her he had a girlfriend. The girl replied and was polite. I wanted to leave him, but he begged me to forgive him. I forgave him, but the infidelity caused a strain in our relationship, and our communication dwindled.

I engaged in a community development course, but he didn't seem pleased. Out of the blue, he asked to move in together in another town. I didn't think it was the best time considering we had a strained relationship and I wanted stability for the children. I thought if the connection failed, I would be the one who would struggle to look for somewhere to live.

I remembered, when I was pregnant with our daughter, I had enrolled in an access course to get to university to do social work. However, due to pregnancy complications, a severe backache and sciatica, it made sitting down or lying down for an extended period uncomfortable. So, I did the course part-time and planned to continue after our daughter was born.

He said he could sort out his work schedule and help me with childcare. However, just before I had our daughter, he said he wanted to go to university to do law. I thought it was random. I took him to an open day at the University where I was studying. He never went to university, and he didn't help with childcare. He claimed he couldn't change his work schedule. I had to juggle the children and my personal development alone. I dropped out of college due to childcare and decided to go back once the children were much older.

One afternoon I was on my way to a course. He called me and said we needed to talk. He said he didn't feel needed in the family because I do what I want to do and I am too westernised. I wasn't like a Kenyan woman. I asked him why, but I got no answer. I told him he was free to do what he wanted as I was only responsible for the choices I made. He told me I overthink things. He said he asked me we move in together or go to Kenya and I had refused. I told him because of the children I couldn't jump into the deep while there was no consistency.

He asked me what I wanted. I told him what I wanted didn't matter if it wasn't what he wanted, but I needed support. He said he wasn't a mind reader to know what I wanted. I told him it wasn't rocket science for him to see the family needed support. I asked him what he wanted, and he said he wanted to be with the family, but I have these principles that I find hard to shift, and I spoil the children. I had told him I didn't like people shouting, smoking or drinking alcohol around the children and if anybody harmed them, I would go to jail.

In February 2008, I left the house, and he followed me and while outside he said he had never seen me in short skirts or wear makeup. I told him I am happy in my skin, and if I wore a sack or a bin bag and walked bare feet, I would still be okay, and I walked away pushing our daughter in a pram.

At the course, my instinct indicated I wouldn't find him at home, and I was right. I didn't bother contacting him because I already knew. However, the hardest thing was when the children asked me where he was. I told them he had left. My five-year-old son asked me whether he had left because they were naughty. I said them it had nothing to do with them; it was his choice and they seemed to take it in well.

I texted him to find out whether he was all right, but I got no reply. Later, I received letters for him from debt companies and never opened them, but when I received a big brown envelope from Kenya, I opened it. I didn't know whether he was dead or alive. I found an invoice from a supermarket amounting to about six hundred pounds. I looked at the things bought and noticed diapers. It boggled my mind.

Before Christmas in 2008, I received a Christmas card from him with his telephone number asking me to call him. I ignored it, but when I received another letter from Kenya from a woman saying he had abandoned her with a five-month old baby in November 2008 and left her with debts, and bailiffs were looking to seize goods from their hotel business, I thought I had to ring him.

I contacted the woman, and she gave me the full story. She wasn't aware of our daughter and me.

I called him and calmly inquired where he had been. He said he had left to clear his head. I asked him whether he was with another woman or had a son he didn't know about. He said I say things that come out of my head and he didn't know where all that was coming from. I told him whatever is hidden in the dark comes to light somehow. He asked what I meant, and I read the letter from the woman, and he went silent. When I questioned him, he said he didn't know what to say.

I remained in touch with the woman and gave her his number. After some time I let him see our daughter. She couldn't recognize him. He asked me to provide him with the last chance, but I ended up being the go-between him and the woman, and it became draining. He asked me to change my number as he had changed his so that the woman couldn't contact me, but I refused.

We ended up not talking for some time, but he came back to the family. However, I couldn't look at him the same way. It made my blood boil and one day I asked him to leave. He threatened me and said I would regret it and that I would have to call the police because of what he would do. I told him I didn't need the police because I would deal with him. My children were asleep. I told him I didn't want noise. He said I have more pride than the British people just because I have citizenship. I told him I am proud of myself because I didn't need a man to get it. He finally left fuming.

I heard from him a few times. During this time, I struggled financially. I remember one time the children and I had to search for coins around the house to buy food. When I asked him to pay fees for our daughter's extracurricular activities, he disappeared. I didn't hear from him for over three years.

However, when at the citizen advice bureau, I saw a child support leaflet. I had seen he had a daughter with another woman and photos with his stepdaughter on Facebook. I wrote to the woman about the children he had abandoned and copied the same message to him, but they both didn't respond.

I contacted the child support agency and gave his details. A few days later he was found. The agency told me the process but said they had to speak to him first. They said I could decide with him or they could take the money off him, but there was a cost. They said they had to put into consideration his expenditure and the children he was taking care of and I know he lied so that he could pay less. He told the agency he would spend the extra money and bought our daughter clothes, but this never happened. However, he maintained what was set by the agency. Money wasn't the issue but consistency, honesty and being there for our daughter.

He asked to see her, and I let him see her twice in my presence. On the third occasion, he asked to take her to his home. I told him it wasn't a good idea to introduce her to a stepfamily before building a relationship with her and hell broke loose. He argued he had a right as her father. I asked him whether he had forgotten those rights when he left or whether it was about the little child support he was paying.

He threatened to take me to court. I received a mediation letter, but he attended before me despite him telling me not to miss the meeting. I was frustrated because I had to take time off from university work placement. I questioned the mediator because I was in the dark and she wasn't impartial. She told me he wanted to have contact with his daughter and I told her I had never refused him. I wanted him to build a relationship with her. She said to me if we didn't agree the case would go to court.

I asked the mediator where he was for over three years if he was such a great dad and if he was supporting his son. I told her I would recommend what my daughter wanted and her best interest. I said if they wanted to take the case to court, it was the best option because I would speak my piece.

The next letter I received from the mediator stated the case was closed, but I could go to court. I felt he was the one who had brought up the issue, and he chickened out. I figured the mediator might have realized there was more than he had disclosed. After that, I didn't hear from him for some time.

Our daughter did finally go to his house, but she didn't want to go. He doesn't cater to her needs or contact her regularly. Being a father is not only about having face-to-face contact but also being there emotionally and providing for her requirements.

After the cancer diagnosis, our daughter informed him about my condition as she was worried. Instead of being supportive, he complained I should be the one telling him. He said he wanted our daughter to be with him two days a week as he did not want her to be with strangers. But she refused as she did not want to be away from me.

I told him to stop talking as if I was dying. He said he did not care about my condition or whether I hated him. All he cared about was our daughter. I told him he should have thought about that a long time ago and I do not dislike him regardless of what he did. I told him what he said was rich coming from a person who had said he wanted to help with the children and also had said I was a strong woman and a good mother.

I had previously asked him to lend me some money, and he told me he would rather throw the money away when I did not agree with his demands regarding our daughter. I told him leopards never change their spots. And now he is all friendly again asking about my condition and wanting to see me. My daughter did once ask him why we split up, and he said he made a few mistakes, which he regrets. At least he didn't blame me.

I have gone through six rounds of chemotherapy and other cancer treatments. Despite this, the medication has not worked because the tumors are back, but I am still on treatment. My greatest fear is to leave my children without a mother. Nevertheless, I believe adversities are meant to strengthen me, and I will keep on striving to get better and reach my goal. It might not be today, but it will happen someday.

KEY LEARNING

1. I believe every challenge in life serves a purpose in someone's life. The trials are meant to strengthen us and set us to a different level.

2. The challenges have made me stronger

3. I have realised that regardless of what we have gone through God has a purpose for all of us, even when it looks dismal. He wouldn't give me something to carry that he was not sure I could endure.

4. My kids have been my best gift and I wouldn't trade it.

ABOUT NATASHA GORDON

Natasha Gordon was born in Islington to Trinidadian parents. She has one younger sister. From the age of two, Natasha grew up in Tottenham, North London. She got married to Jermaine Gordon and has five children between them, including her nephew who now lives with them.

Natasha is an Antenatal Practitioner for the National Childbirth Trust. She helps new parents to deepen their knowledge of pregnancy and the physiology of birth and supports them through their incredible journey of parenthood. Natasha is responsible for developing and teaching "Birth and Beyond" courses and facilitates discussions and group work.

Natasha also practices Kinesiology and helps postnatal woman correct imbalances within their body. The sessions explore their feelings around stress, self-awareness, anxiety and low moods; she aims to increase their energy and social wellness; certainty and decision making, self-respect and confidence. Natasha can detect the root cause/s behind the symptoms by using a muscle test procedure and a range of treatments including lymphatic massage, electrical balancing, nutrition and emotional work.

Before starting as a Practitioner, Natasha ran three successful businesses. She still works part-time at Gordons Group Property Services alongside her husband, who builds and transforms properties, creating comfort for living.

Natasha also accomplished and managed a top-branded, exclusive wellbeing salon for 15 years, which was awarded for quality customer service and care. After a successful career servicing well-known professionals, Natasha came across the opportunity to co-author the book 'Single Woman's Anthology' and now reveals the story of a single mother called Carella who fights for her fairy-tale ending after facing torture and pain from a narcissistic relationship breakup.

#Every child deserves a great start

#say no to relationship conflict

#get help early

E:natashagordon64@yahoo.com

SINGLERELLA - LOVE LIFTS HER UP WHERE SHE BELONGS

At the hospital, Carella's goal was to have a natural birth without any pain relief apart from the gas and air. She hoped that after having her baby, she and Kendal would rekindle their relationship and raise their baby in a loving home.

It was about 6 am, on a hot summer's day. After a few hours of taking the gas and air, the contractions became more intense, and the midwife instructed Carella to try something stronger. She was ultimately against having an epidural due to previous back problems, so she opted for Pethidine, which was a huge mistake.

Kendal was there looking on from a distance, sickened at what he saw. The midwife explained, "Your baby is in distress we need to push this labour along now". The pain and after effects were impressing her and she yelled out "Give me that epidural!!!" The room was becoming noisier, as everyone drew closer. The midwife directed Carella to push, but she was not pushing at the right time. She blurted out "I cannot feel my legs, I feel numb." "I cannot do this!!" She cried.

Then just as she felt like giving up, she heard a cry.

Kendal stared at Carella in total disgust. There was horror all over his face, and without any remorse, he spat out the words cold-bloodedly ..."IT'S OVER!" Carella went silent trying to analyse what she just heard.

Unaware of what he said, the midwife excitedly hollered, "It's a girl!" The nurse placed her gently on Carella's chest. Her tiny, helpless hands were grasping on Carella's breast, and Carella gently wrapped her arms securely around her.

Carella never expected that on the day she gave birth her whole life was going to alter in minutes completely. She knew that working things out with Kendal wasn't going to be easy. But as usual, she was hoping or believing that good things will happen in the future.

The effects of the pethidine (a potent pain reliever drug which was injected directly into a muscle of Carella's buttock) had left her very drowsy, nauseous, tired, and spaced out.

Her attention drifted onto her childhood dream that was inspired by her favourite story Cinderella, who met a marvelous prince that swept her off her feet. Carella always felt that despite her unpleasant childhood experiences that one day she would get married only once to a handsome and very kind man, have beautiful children and live forever happy.

A tear dropped as it was the first time she felt so vulnerable and dependant on Kendal. As she looked up at him, his eyes clenched as he hastily said: "my mother is coming over in a few weeks". "Oh" she replied in surprise; "your mother didn't mention this to me". He angrily hauled, "you are lucky... my mother is lighting candles for you". Carella's eyes became heavy with tears and gradually closed shut. She took three deep breaths but was gasping for air. The room was becoming hotter, and there were not any fans in the room.

Twenty-four hours later, a new-born physical examination was done; the doctor said that Kaye had jaundice which was high levels of a substance called bilirubin in her blood.

At that point, Carella was all alone, her palms felt sweaty, and although tired she anxiously asked the doctor, "What is the treatment?"

The doctor calmly explained that Kaye would start phototherapy treatment as soon as possible using a special blue-green light to break down the bilirubin stored in her skin. The phototherapy unit would be set up by her bedside. All this new information felt utterly foreign to Carella as she opened her bible for comfort.

After one week in the hospital, Carella was finally discharged. Kaye was feeling better. She even saw her smile for the first time.

Carella quickly packed up all their belongings as she waited for Kendal to arrive. Not long after she could see Kaye opening and closing her mouth, she seemed ready again for her milk, so Carella took her out of the cot and breastfed her as she proudly stroked Kaye's beautiful face. A few moments later, Kendal arrived. Carella hesitantly said "I will be 5 minutes," but he was in a hurry, picked up Kaye's bag and walked back down the corridor.

Luckily the nurse who had been looking after them for that week came over to say goodbye, so Carella quickly asked her for a spare nappy and some cotton balls to change Kaye soiled nappy, which resembled mustard and cottage cheese mixed with lots of little seed-like specks.

The journey home was quiet. Carella attempted to make conversation saying, "We need to get Kaye registered," Kendal responded. "Can't you go?" I think we both need to be there, she replied.

During the silence, as Carella looked through the car window, she admired a couple happily walking together with their kids, and she inwardly thought 'I wonder when the Cinderella in me will find my happy moment'.

That night Carella emerged into her double bed and the word "IT'S OVER" began to replay in her mind. She remembered when they first met; Kendal made it known how attracted he was to her. He went out of his way to pursue her attention and was so proud to introduce her to his family and friends. Then, they used to have so much fun, listening to the same music, similar cultures and tastes for food. Within the first six months of their relationship, Kendal was already planning their future together. He would talk about going on holidays, having children, getting married and starting business ventures together. At first, Carella felt their relationship was moving too fast, but then Kendal's constant fantasies of success became something to look forward to. Unfortunately, Carella's family, particularly her mother, didn't seem to share the same joy. Her mother tipped her off about him, but she ignored her warning and wanted to prove her parents wrong about her first relationship.

After all, Carella was young, working two jobs a day, living independently plus she was still doing some part time study while dating Kendal. Kendal was also hard working with a motive to excel in life. So Carella couldn't see why her parents felt so upset with her. A year later she put plans in place to start her own business.

Kendal and Carella had been together for seven years of her young life. They had many conversations about the future but had not spoken about what they would do in the event of an unplanned pregnancy. The last thing Carella wanted was to have a child out of wedlock. It was something she seriously feared and knew if it ever happened that way, she would feel culturally disappointed with herself because marriage first was essential to her.

In the first year of Carella's business, she became pregnant and feared to tell her parents. Deep down thoughts about her relationship with Kendal began to raise questions in her mind because when she announced the news to him, everything seemed to change between them.

On reflection, she wondered, did everything change then? Or before?

It was approaching midnight when Kendal fled into the house and slammed the front door shut. BANG!! Carella was breastfeeding Kaye when she heard Kendal scrambling up the stairs. Without warning, he barged into her bedroom waving a piece of paper in his hand. Within moments he grabbed Kaye from Carella's breast and dumped her in her moses basket and shouted, "You need to sign this for the house," as soon as Carella reluctantly signed, Kendal rushed out the room and out of the house, shouting, "You just signed away your rights to your house fool!"

Disappointment and sadness shadowed across her face. Uncontrollable tears flooded her face as she said her nightly prayers with her eyes wide open.

The next few weeks were awkward; all attention was on Kaye, and very few words were exchanged. The mortgage company confirmed that everything was still up to date.

When Kendal's mother arrived, Carella tried to maintain her usual welcoming manner. She greeted her with Kaye in her arms holding a hello grandma balloon. His mother didn't comment on it but was very excited to see her first granddaughter and cherished every moment with her. Although there was a strange silence between them, she set a routine for Kaye that was favoured.

No words were exchanged about the difficulties that Kendal and Carella were having and Carella knew somehow that she wasn't going to discuss it. She was only in London for one week to spend time with her granddaughter.

FIVE WEEKS LATER

One early morning as Carella was doing her usual duties she suddenly felt intense cramps digging her lower belly that would not stop. In a matter of seconds, she felt faint and dizzy and called out to Kendal who was sitting close. "I don't feel well!!.... My insides feel on fire. Merely able to speak she told Kendal to call the ambulance. He looked her right in the eyes and completely refused as he watched her fall to the floor. Somehow despite Carella's lack of response, he managed to get her in his car. On the way to the hospital, she was awoken by the blast of breeze from the air conditioner, but the pain was still unbearable. She staggered alone to the A & E Hospital department, while Kendal found parking. It wasn't long before Carella's name was called. Her breasts were becoming engorged with milk. "Where is Kaye?" she thought. For some strange reason, she knew something was seriously wrong and immediately gained some unforeseen strength allowing her to walk out of the hospital. Approaching her were two white male police officers, on either side of Kendal. "Where is Kaye?" Carella firmly hollered.

The policemen's face was almost beetroot red; Kendal was speechless. Carella shouted, "Where is my baby?" No one could answer. The police officers quickly directed them to the police car; helicopters were circling above. It was apparent something serious had happened to Kaye, so she did as directed then the policemen put the sirens on as they sped off at high speed. At that moment Carella didn't care who was listening and how she sounded. She held on tightly to the side handle and prayed and prayed for God to find her baby. It was Carella's first time praying in this way. Unexpectedly, she remembered one of the first scriptures that she recited in church when she was ten years old. It concerned the discipline of an associated believer who had sinned in the church and needed to be corrected by the congregation accurately.

MATTHEW 18:19-21 NEW KING JAMES VERSION (NKJV)

19 "Again[a] I say to you that if two of you agree on earth concerning anything that they ask, it will be done for them by My Father in heaven. 20 For where two or three are gathered together in my name, I am there in the midst of them."

She then immediately felt the urge to call her mother's friend who began to pray with her on the phone. Carella then said "Dear God, you said in John 14:13 (New International Version)

"And I will do whatever you ask in my name, so that the Father may be glorified in the Son". I then cried out, "My Father if I have never said before, I say now, I am willing to give my life to you, if you bring back my baby safe, unharmed, well and you find the person that took her".

At that point the radio speaker in the police car announced," Baby's been found! Baby's been found!! She is safe, unharmed and well". The policemen were astonished he bawled "this is a miracle!! I believe in your God". Carella was also in shock unaware of how loudly she was praying. Kendal sat in silent shock, and we later found out that Kaye had been handed in by the man who stole Kendal's car. The police officer said he was shocked to witness the man on his knees begging for forgiveness for stealing the car with Kaye in it.

On return to the hospital, Kendal had disappeared. Carella was alone again but happy to have Kaye safely in her arms. The news quickly spread through to the hospital staff about what happened to Kaye. On the way to get a CT scan, Carella met another friend of her mother who was a nurse; she was shocked to hear what had happened and made every effort to speak to the team involved with her care. Reporters were continually calling to get a story, but the incident was too overwhelming to discuss.

A short while later, the doctors explained that there were trapped residues of placenta found inside Carella's uterus and that made her susceptible to infection and even death. Medication and fluid were quickly given to remove the wastes and help the womb to contract, as well as antibiotics to clear up any predisposed infection. Carella was still very dazed and completely shattered but yet very watchful for her daughter's sake.

The following week, Kaye began crying in the late afternoon and every evening for several hours. She was clenching her fists and arching her back while crying extensively. No matter what Carella did, she could not comfort her. Coping with the demands of a new baby on her own as well as everything else that was going on around her was becoming tough as Carella was still very poorly.

Kendal was rarely at home and when he stopped by the atmosphere felt deadly like a cone snail.

The health visitor visited regularly, and she said that little Kaye was suffering from Colic. Carella eagerly tried a range of carefully selected herbal medicines, but nothing seemed to work.

The health visitor also gave her a list of things to try, but there was no change.

Carella was anxious for a good night's sleep; however, she was uncertain about asking for help because she felt embarrassed about the situation, she was in. It was stressful and depressing, and she was pretending to be happy but felt all alone, wrapped up in her tears.

Co- sleeping with Kaye wasn't part of Carella's plan, because some research suggests that sleeping with your baby in a bed or sofa can cause the baby to overheat and suffocate causing an increased risk of sudden infant death syndrome (SIDS). Despite this, Carella's gut instinct was to put Kaye in a well-fitted baby sleeping bag nearer the wall and keep her bedding light. Sleeping in the same bed with Kaye, gave her the chance to check on her through the night. She knew she was doing the right thing and gently stroked her hair until she fell asleep.

No matter what the challenge Carella always put on a brave face to others, particularly her parents and ever shared a smile or encouraging word to others around her. She joined a great church called Fountain of Life Ministry which her mother discovered. Although she had been attending this church for only six months, the church was very supportive of her. When she told her Pastor Rev. C Turner what was happening at home, she immediately suggested Mediation in the presence of herself and another. Carella agreed and was surprised when Kendal showed up for the meeting, but sadly nothing was resolved. Kendal was adamant that Carella was the problem and he accepted no blame for his actions. Another meeting was set up with his relative who felt it was necessary to act as his power of Attorney to discuss selling Carella's share of her home to Kendal. Carella openly objected and put all her frustrations in prayer. Carella had a memory of her late grandma (on Carella's mother's side), which said to her "where there is a beginning, there will always be an end."

Carella's Pastor encouraged her to have a healthy relationship with God and build a prayer life. She learnt more about the Bible and became stronger mentally, physically, and spiritually.

SIX MONTHS LATER

The winter coldness had stormed under the gap of the front door. Carella woke up trembling and starry-eyed with the duvet wrapped tightly around her. She jumped up and turned over in her bed to check on Kaye who was sleeping snuggly in her baby sleeping bag. Carella leant back on her pillow and gently closed her eyes, trying to understand her dream. She could remember some very significant parts of her vision and the natural part of her felt there was a message through this dream.

In her dream, there was a road direction sign pointing right with the destination, South Norwood written boldly. Then the dream switched and she saw a building. Inside the building were a team of builders doing a complete refurbishment to a specific standard. Above the building were flats. She saw Kendal looking at these flats and wasn't sure why, but he seemed to have a special connection to this building.

That week Kendal phoned and said "we need to have a business meeting on Thursday" which was in two days. He did not ask about Kaye. Kendal's voice and manner were solemn, almost as if he hardly knew her. He demanded, "I need a projection of the figures for the last three months". Carella was gob-smacked because it had been nearly two years since the business had been opened and Kendal never brought any meat to the table. This was officially Carella's business. She legally purchased it for a hefty sum which was paid to his relative who was retiring. Carella solely managed and leased the property through an independent firm and registered Kendal as a director because he was her partner at the time. Kendal expected to be a director as he freely stated 'it was once his family's businesses. "

She didn't give his comments too much attention at the time as she thought Carella was getting a discount off the premium because of his family connection. However, she later learnt that this was not true. When she first bought the business, they were both very pleased. Kendal had some excellent ideas and spoke enthusiastically. The business name was changed, and a new sign was fitted.

Carella's close friends and family supported her with improving the business outlook, such as cleaning, painting and decorating, fitting some new wooden flooring and repositioning furniture. Some of the previous staff was not asked to stay on as their work ethics were not what was required. As a result, many of the old clients followed those staff, and the business became more vibrant and professional.

When Kaye was born, the business was in full swing. Carella had to still manage the day-to-day business, accounts, staff and her private life.

Her pregnancy fat dropped off her like well-cooked meat leaves the bone, and on her return back to work it was becoming apparent to the staff that something was wrong.

Carella often brought baby Kaye with her to the business for the first six months, as she was still breastfeeding and had to visit the business twice a week on foot to ensure everything was running smoothly. Her team was very hard working, loyal and supportive to her and Kaye. They were keen to hold Kaye and play with her, and she enjoyed it while Carella tried to quickly observe the shop floor, have one-to-one meetings, and make orders for required stock.

Carella was very fortunate that when she returned to work, a friend of her mother was willing to come to her home and give Kaye good quality childcare. She also helped her with household duties, prepare meals for Kaye, and bathe her before she returned. She may have suspected Carella's pains of disappointment with Kendal, but she never shared this with her.

It was springtime, the fresh breeze was blowing, and the cold winter air was still present. Weeks went by, and Kendal was reluctant to see Kaye. Carella wished that he would collect his belongings from the wardrobe, which was filled with nearly new clothes; so, she could be released from his passive aggression. Whenever he passed by to pick up Kaye for the day, he was always wearing a new set of clothes and designer sunglasses and silently shunned her when she asked about collecting his clothes. In the evening when he returned, Kaye's food, and drinks were brought back untouched. He was gone before she could ask when Kaye had last eaten. She could only guess that Kaye ate whatever he ate and he enjoyed doing things his way.

One wet afternoon, when Carella was on her way back home, Kaye was in the pushchair, but the rain was beating down on the pushchair rain cover. Carella was struggling to keep up her umbrella as the ghastly wind was forcing her umbrella to turn outwards. When they finally arrived at the doorstep, she was anxious to get Kaye inside and change her wet, cold trousers and take off her shoes. She stretched for her keys at the bottom of her bag and hassled to open the lock. The key was sticking and didn't seem to fit. She tried it again. It took a few moments before she realised that the locks had been changed and she could not get into her house. She knew Kendal was not manually skilled so someone he knew must have willingly changed the locks for him.

Carella reached for her phone, unsure who to call or what to do. She reluctantly called her mother as she looked at Kaye, who slowly flickered her eyes and then closed her eyes to sleep as she snuggled under her soft, warm fleece with her mitts and hat. There was no answer. As Carella looked up, she saw Kendal from a distance walking towards the house. As he got closer, he looked at her with a mocking smirk on his face. This made Carella furious, and she began to yell at him, uncontrollably. He made it evident that he was angrier than her and became hostile and abusive. Without hesitation, she called the police because Kendal was becoming violent, threatening and insulting.

Kendal slammed the front door open. The force hit the wall aggressively. Carella was still distraught and shouted, "Kaye was sleeping! What is wrong with you?" Kendal charged at her collaring her against the wall with his clawing hands. He was shocked when the police arrived within minutes and individually carried out their investigations. They treated this as a civil matter and would not take it further because the house was in joint names; therefore, according to what they said, both parties were both entitled to change the locks. The police officers stated that a breach of the peace had or would occur and gave Kendal a caution warning. Which meant he could be arrested if he refused to resolve the matter? They suggested that either Kendal leave the first of the double doors unlocked or he gave Carella a set of keys. Kendal decided to go the first of the two external front doors opened as he had a key for the second front door.

Carella was not happy and was scared that not only was her home at risk of burglary, but there was a risk of invalidating her home insurance. She decided to call a locksmith to change the first external door lock, but not long after, Kendal changed the locks again. Luckily Carella received a phone call from victim support, which was referred to her by another organisation through the police outsources. They decided that they would supply and fit a new front door with new insurance safe security locks.

This made a significant difference, and Carella felt very safe for a while; and focused on bringing up Kaye.

Kaye was still not sleeping through the night, and she was exasperated and fussy through the days but could not rest appropriately as they were mostly together while Carella had to be in the shop every day. Carella was always well groomed, but her clothes size had dropped from 10 to 6. Luckily the stress did not massively impact on her breastfeeding as she managed to establish great attachment and bonding with Kaye very early after birth and Kaye was demanding breast milk regularly. Breastfeeding gave Carella and Kaye quality time together and helped her escape from what was going on.

At times Carella felt a little overwhelmed and didn't like to see housework build up. Although it was challenging running a home and doing the day-to-day shopping with a young baby on her own, she refused to see herself as a single mother.

Every evening she wrote in her prayer diary the things she needed to accomplish. Marriage was vital to her from an early age, and she told God daily that she needed a husband who was a believer of Jesus. A husband that would love and care for her and Kaye, who would be able to fix things and help around the house, whose mother loved God and most of all she wanted to share her life with someone who respected her and her parents.

Growing up, it was always her intention to get married before having children, as it was a family cultural belief. When this did not happen, she felt humiliated and embarrassed that her relationship with Kendal did not work out. Her mother always commented and believed that Kendal was not the right person for her, but she did not want to listen and now she felt like zero when her mother was right. It was challenging for her to return to her mother for any help, mainly as she was not in support of her relationship with Kendal from the beginning. Carella knew she needed extra support from her parents. It was offered, but she had chosen not to take it. Her parents were always willing to do whatever she asked if not more.

ONE YEAR AFTER KAYE WAS BORN

Carella had returned to work almost full-time. Some of the days she worked were quite long as she was in a hectic season. On her days off, the staff informed her that they witnessed Kendal helping himself to the till which occasionally left the till short.

She confronted Kendal about the missing money, but Kendal was very angry with her for confronting him, it was almost confusing. He dragged her up on one of the discreet back walls behind the shop, threating to finish her off. She called the police in fright but later tried to abort the call because she was ashamed and frightened about anyone in the business knowing what was happening.

Things started to get worse as he began to arrange secret meetings with the staff outside the business and was offering incentives.

Carella later found out that he had opened a similar business within a 5-mile radius of hers and his new girlfriend was running it. It was all starting to make sense when news came back to Carella that he was living in South Norwood with his new girlfriend and the building that was being refurbished in her dream was his new business which shockingly had flats above it.

Six months after Kendal's business had opened, he ran into difficulty and pleaded for Carella's help. He had asked his girlfriend to leave and presented a business proposition to Carella concerning his shop. As an act of kindness, Carella was prepared to help him and park her matters to one side temporarily. Although he looked desperate, she was not willing to accept his business proposition to add Carella's name to his business and partner as a sister company.

Carella visited the business and met an old school friend whose partner was working in the business. She instantly felt obliged to look out for her and discovered she was connected to others she knew. Within a week Carella caught site of a bailiff letter to forfeit goods, which were to be removed the next day. Some of the team were already aware and were frightened as some of their goods were at the property.

That evening Carella spoke to Devon who was one of the Head Barbers from her business. He was always supportive and offered to help her clear the premises. Kendal did not turn up as he said, he couldn't get out of work to assist with removing the goods from his shop but supplied a large box van with a tail lift.

His staff stayed late with Carella and Devon to help load the van until early hours of the morning. It was surprising how much things had to be removed.

Carella managed to organise storage with a local company that required her to fill out a contract. In the desperate need to secure room she registered her details and expected Kendal to pay for it. Unfortunately, he never paid so she stopped paying and all goods were seized.

Just before this time, Carella received a business loan of £10,000 to refurbish her shop. This was paid into the business saving account which was still in joint names with Kendal. When she received her quarterly bank statement, which was after Kendal's business had elapsed, she stared at it in shock for maybe 20 minutes or more. There were lots of debit transactions. She did not recognise any of them. She noticed a code after each transaction and immediately contacted the bank, and the bank clerk explained that the code was the last four digits of the bank card that was used. He confirmed that this bankcard belonged to Kendal. She was steaming mad.

There was nothing left, and the loan had to be repaid. The shop had not even been refurbished yet, and the staff and clients were expecting the shop to be closed for a few weeks for refurbishment. The bank clerk explained that as it was a joint loan, both parties were both legally and liable for repayment of this loan. She advised Carella to contact the citizen's advice bureau for further advice. Unfortunately, things got progressively worse, a few months later the whole shop was stripped of its contents leaving only a mannequin head standing in the middle of the shop floor. Customers had reported back that they had seen a large lorry and a team of men removing all the goods, fittings, sinks in the early hours of the morning from Carella's shop. They presumed that the shop was being refurbished and was disturbed to hear what had happened. Carella contacted the police immediately, and Kendal was arrested for possession of dumping her passport and salon goods in someone's back garden and for suspicion of robbing her shop. After such a long process they let him go, and the matter was treated as a civil matter again because the business was in joint names.

Carella later found out that the form she had signed was for a secured loan against the house for £10000 to support his business venture. The company stated that because they had received Carella's passport as ID and signature they approved the secured loan and they could not remove Carella's name.

It had now been just over a year since the relationship ended. Carella was becoming very ill and couldn't hold down any food because the stress was becoming too much. She reasoned with God to untangle her from this web. She could not take his persistent harassment anymore. Her daughter needed her, and so did her business. This was her primary source of income, and she was feeling financially and emotionally exhausted. Kendal was no longer providing anything for Kaye or towards her upkeep. Carella continued to pray.

Carella had excellent contacts with salon furniture suppliers who loaned her some furniture for a monthly cost. Some of her staff resigned as they were frightened and worried about their job security. Carella just kept praying for change according to Hebrews 11: Faith in God changes everything. She remembered a sermon in church about faith, explaining that "faith is the evidence of things not seen." Hebrews 11:1. Her pastor shared some great examples: 'You cannot see air, but you can't live without it. We cannot see love and peace, but it's embedded in our hearts'. Carella believed that having faith in God was going to bring about change for the better and it was coming soon.

Victim support contacted Carella again and referred her to an organisation called National domestic violence which has a 24-hour Freephone Helpline. This organisation had links to other charity-based organisations that supported her in preparing an application for an injunction to prohibit Kendal from harassing, annoying or entering her home or business. The court granted an injunction order against Kendal. He also signed an undertaking at the court to promise the court he would not come within a set distance to Carella. The court also granted for the house to be sold and all the loans to be paid from the proceeds of the sale.

When Kaye was one year and six months old, God finally revealed Carella's Prince. It was Devon. For some reason, he made her blush uncontrollably. He was naturally always there for her whenever she hit hard times; he always had a perfect solution. But Carella never suspected that he was her prince. It was imperative to Carella that her future husband was neat, tidy, and able to fix things intelligently around the house as well as have a good job." Carella began to look back on all the other disasters that had happened in the salon and then she realised that Devon was always there for her. When she first got the shop a few months after, a car drove right through the middle of the shop; Devon was the first at the scene to help with the investigations. There was a fire in Carella's shop, and all the walls were black; he arranged with some staff to clean the walls and repaint them. When the salon washing machine stopped working, he fixed it. The toilet wasn't flushing; he unblocked it with his bare hands. There was a flood of water coming from the upstairs flat into Carella's shop, near the electrics, and he protected all the plug sockets and stopped the leak in the apartments above. The ceiling tile cracked and fell onto Carella, which caused an injury to her arm. Devon immediately took out the first aid kit, cleaned and dressed her wound.

As the conversation between them flowed and time went on, she discovered that his mother is a Bishop and a powerful God-fearing woman of God. Devon loves The Lord Jesus and naturally built a stable relationship with Kaye. It was becoming clear that he was her angel sent by God. This was one of Carella's third revelations. There were no doubts that God is real. She learnt that God honestly answers prayers and it only happens at the right time when we genuinely believe. Carella earnestly continued to pray even more as she wanted to be 100% sure this was the man that God had intended for her to marry.

She believed with all her heart that God was able to find the right husband for her. She was not prepared to settle for less. She wanted a man of God.

After six months of being together, the army called upon him to go to Afghanistan. Carella was devastated, but hid in prayer and told God "if he is the one for me why are you sending him away? If he is the one for me, please bring him back and let us get married heavenly father, in Jesus name I pray." It was improbable that Devon was going to return, the army seemed dead set on him going. Carella arranged a leaving party for him but was still hoping that he would not have to go.

The time had come for them to say goodbye. It was happening, but she continued to pester God in her quiet corner literally. Before leaving the UK, all soldiers had to go through pre-travel safety measures and carry out the necessary paperwork. They both spoke daily and shared jokes and recognised each other for the great individuals they were. They both experienced sleepless nights thinking of each other and anticipated seeing each other soon.

It wasn't long after that something magical happened. Devon said he was coming home; Carella was in complete shock and amazement because she couldn't understand how this was possible, and neither did he. However, she knew it was God's work, and she was happy. It was clear that God had sent an Angel to sort it all out.

Carella began to understand the journey she had encountered. It was almost like an intensive course of life lessons to correct her path and teach her never to love anyone or anything more than God. Carella realised that everything was in place when she did it God's way.

Not long after her angel Devon became her prince charming, they made plans to get married and the wedding day was filled with love and laughter. They later had a son and daughter together, and Kaye was loved as his daughter. Devon also had a daughter called Jane who was slightly older, and she made our family complete.

Eventually, Carella's shop was refurbished before she got married. Devon surprised her by taking out a loan of £10K and renovated her shop himself. Carella managed to secure the business in her name because everything that Kendal did to Carella turned around for her good in the end. To this day Carella's husband buys her these impressive unique slippers and they are always a perfect fit.

KEY LEARNING

Whilst writing my chapter, I realised that I could no longer supress my painful memories. As I put pencil to paper I felt the hurts and disappointments gradually fade away. It was at this time I valued the gift of forgiving myself and others.

During my journey of healing I cried out to God to help me, save me, heal me. I was broken, unsure of my life, scared and alone with a young baby to raise. I desperately needed change. It was at that point I built a divine connection with God and my paths gradually became clearer.

I learnt to speak to God first about all things and to trust in him fully. I became slow to act and quick to listen.

Today I am very thankful to God for turning my life around. I am blessed with a wonderful caring husband and a beautiful family. Our journey together hasn't been easy but each experience has been a great lesson which has made me a better wife, mother and daughter.

ABOUT EVEANA SHACARA HENRY

"Talk di tings dem!" … A phrase made popular by a very special, talented and ambitious young lady from the 'village' of Kingston, Jamaica. Eveana Henry, also known as 'Pamputtae' was known in her community as 'Buju' or 'Buju Fabulous', as the name of her crew was 'Fabulous Girls'. This Gemini, born June 19, 1985, attended the Calabar All Age School where she realized her obvious talent for dancing and music. She came from humble beginnings as a resident of 'Gulf' in Fletchers Land. At the age of 10, Pamputtae's mother passed away, leaving her with her sister, grandmother and aunt. Her sister and grandmother passed away soon after. This was a very sad time in Eveana's life; however, she did not give up her quest for stardom. Pamputtae's big break came in 2006 when she did an intro for Tony Matterhorn for his song 'Goodas Fi Dem'. The song was an instant hit, which took Pamputtae's name all over the world. At the 2008 staging of Fully Loaded and Beenie Man's Summer Sizzle, Pamputtae gave an excellent performance, earning her many a 'forwards' and rave reviews in the print media. "I love the African movies and I would always say "Hey! Pamputtae!" so soon after the intro with Matterhorn, the fans and some friends of mine said that's the name I should use. So, from that, the name just stuck." Business was the name of the game for Pamputtae as she did some work in the studio and released 'It Good' on the Trash Out Riddim for Good Yute Productions in 2007. With her song being a regular on popular radio stations, she soon after did a collaboration called 'Talk Di Tings Dem' on the Slacker's Riddim. The song quickly became a club favourite. Also included in her catalogue of songs is 'Queen In A Di Ring', released by Swatch Int'l.

Pamputtae, determined, focused and humble, aims to create waves on the dancehall scene. For Pamputtae, the journey continues…

THE JUGGLE

My name is Eveana Shacara Henry but most people would know me by my dancehall artiste/stage name "PAMPUTTAE". I hailed from the city of Kingston, Jamaica in a community called Fletchers Land. Life was very rough for my mother who was also a "Single Mother". I once attended Calabar Junior High School, which was difficult for my mother who couldn't provide for me most of the things I needed. My Father was locked away in a United States Federal Prison so it was really hard for my Mother alone. Things were bad but got worse when she passed away when I was only ten years of age, leaving behind me and my sister, who passed away a few years after. At this time I had to live with my Aunt and my Grandmother who were both struggling to make two ends meet. I encountered a lot of peer pressure and depression, when what I really needed was some comfort and help. My school journey was also challenging, because my Aunt and my Grandmother couldn't provide enough on the table. So I went astray. I met my first baby father and gave birth to my first child at the age of fifteen and was thrown out of school. The struggles got worse because my baby father could not provide all the necessities that a baby mother would need during and after pregnancy. During my pregnancy, there were a lot of times that I never had anything to eat, I desired food that I couldn't afford and I had to eat what I had. I realized when I was too late, I got a reality check. I could remember going on the road to beg for twenty dollars to buy diapers for my baby. I prayed for days and nights for a miracle and finally my wish was granted. I met a lady name Jackey. She helped me a lot by registering me in a women's center to enable me to further my education, but it didn't work out in my favor. It was very difficult for me to pay bus fare to go school and provide diapers, baby food and food for myself. I had to quit school and start selling rags in the busy streets of downtown Kingston. I had to bring my son along with me, and I put him in a cardboard box to gain my hustle. This was really going the wrong way; my baby got sick because of the dust blowing on the road side where I was selling. Seeking a job, I got my first official job at the Gleaner Company of Jamaica, which gave me experience at the time as a "Single Mother" and took care of all my baby needs. I got another job in which we were packing Codfish/Salt fish in boxes for distribution.

Me, Eveana Shacara Henry, didn't know that being a single mother and going through the struggles that I had would allow me to become a Reggae Artiste. I got introduced to Tony Matteron - that's how I got the name Pamputtae - and I started to move away from all the previous struggles from the past. I got the name Pamputtae from a song intro I did for Tony Matteron called "Goddas Fi Dem". The name was taken from an African film. The song went viral in the dancehall market and took me to a level where I accumulated a lot more hit songs that earned me the name "Fluffy Diva Pamputtae". I gained more recognition when I did the song with female dancehall artiste "Spice" called "Slim Gal vs. Fluffy Gal". It took me to the next level in the dancehall. I changed the way a Jamaican would look at a fat woman especially in the dancehall. I also gave a lot of courage to fat women in the Jamaican dancehall and at parties. It only took a few weeks for the change to occur - it went from Fat to Fluffy. For a musician/single mother, things were looking awesome and I had everything under total control emotionally and financially until I got pregnant again, this time by a married man. My relationship with my second child father wasn't so bad but as time passed things started to get rough and here comes reality again.

I thought that it was a perfect time to be settled with my second child father, so we lived together. Everything was fine during my pregnancy however I had a few challenges because I never wanted my music career to deteriorate. During my pregnancy, I continued with my recording sessions in the studio and continued to travel for show/gigs overseas. I got discouragement from someone I never expected it from - my second child father. I noticed my second child father, the man that I lived with, start to discourage me about my music career. He would utter words like "Your music is rubbish", "You are not going to be a successful musician", "There is no place for you in music" and "They are only foolish songs you can't sing". I tried to avoid all the negative thoughts and energy but there was trouble around the corner that I knew nothing about.

Problems arose when the second baby father's previous baby mother decided to give us some trouble although they had broken up. The situation got worse when his mother got involved and was on the next baby mother's side. His wife got involved along with other family members and it was a total chaos for me. There were days that we would have endless arguments, which led me to have headaches most of the time. It was one single mother against one entire family. At this point in my life I never thought of anything worse that could possibly happen to me but my guess was wrong; it wasn't over yet. My baby father, who I was living with, slept with my neighbor next door and I found out. I realized at this point I had a decision to make that would impact my life and my kids forever. I was premeditating how to murder both my second child father and the neighbor, but when I thought about my freedom and my children's future, I told him we had to separate and so we did. I guess sometimes the Almighty Father God has to break our heart to save our soul and you got to let go of some people to grow. Although we weren't living together anymore, I sent over our son to visit him on the weekends and when our son would return, he gave him no lunch money, so I decided to stop sending him over to visit. I remember one day he told me that "what is good for the goose is good for the gander". That means the same way he treats me is the same way he will treat our son.

When the single mother struggle really hit me is when I realized that it was only me, my kids and Almighty God alone. There was a time going up to that point where I heard a whispering in the wind that said "Hang your self", and I contemplated suicide. I was very strong within me to know that I couldn't do that to my children and me.

My story was unheard for years until I was called upon by a record label named Wopen Door Records to produce a cultural reggae song. With so many struggles with single mothers around the world including myself, I decided to do a single mother song. The song was written by me, Eveana, and Esco a writer, singer and producer from Kingston, Jamaica. The single mother song picked up a buzz the first week it was published on social media. The record label decided to go ahead with the video, so we had a great visual that depicts the true levity and struggle of a single mother. The audiovisual went worldwide; the feedback was and is presently awesome. International Hip-hop artiste Foxy Brown reached out on my Instagram page publicly. The single mother song is very emotional and it captivates every single mother who has heard the song. The comments on social media are so touching that it causes a lot of single mothers to cry. I would see comments like "Tears are running down my face now and I am not a single mother but I see my friend going through single mother struggles". My single mother song doesn't only have an impact on a single mother but also a child with only a mother or a mother without a father, and the list goes on.

I founded a single mother foundation to help out single mothers to prevent situations that they had experienced in the past. I am grateful to the companies, organizations and individuals who support the single mother foundation to help single mothers in need. The single mother struggle is present today but by the aid of the Almighty God, He will see us through, and after a storm there will be a calm.

KEY LEARNING

1. My hardest times lead to the greatest moments of my life. I kept going! The tough situations built a strong woman in the end.

2. Where you think you lack the ability to succeed that's where your biggest opportunities lie. Just keep on trusting God.

3. My kids were sent to teach me lessons of love, patience, and resilience.

MARRIED BUT DOING IT ALONE!

I found myself in the back of an ambulance, and all I could think of was where was my son Mikhel Kai? It was now time for him to be collected from the nursery, and I was being transported to Mayday hospital in London. At that moment, my first reaction was to reach for my phone and call the nursery to say I was running late, but in reality, I wasn't going to make it. How would I tell them this without the fear of social services on my case?

The ambulance staff called his father, who told them he had a meeting and could not leave.

So I scurried around frantically trying to find a person passing by who could pick up my son from nursery. I was doing all this because I know I was going to be held at the hospital for some time.

** That was just a reminder that although I had been a mother for almost 21 years, I have done it alone for over 18 years.

You see I have been married twice one I don't recognise as a marriage.

However, in the eyes of the law I was married.

When I met the second husband, my first child from the first marriage was ten years old.

I was finished with the having kids pretty much and didn't want to be a single mother anymore.

The path had been too challenging especially living in the UK with no help socially or emotionally. There was absolutely no respite.

I struggled as a mother and parent to provide and do so many other bits. When my daughter had one of her terrible breakdowns, I remember I was on the way to the hospital where she was going to undergo general anaesthetics, and I was on BBC radio doing an interview.

She had a panic attack, and I was live on air. I was also driving and so confused about what to do. Luckily the phone call was on my headset. She started panicking, and I wanted to cut the interview. One glimpse at her and she signalled for me to stay on the call. I was so confused as it came suddenly based on an argument she had with her father, now truthfully, I think the scare of the surgery she was about to undergo on her eye also made her stressed. It was compounded as her father was meant to accompany her and he didn't. She felt let down by him again, and she had a meltdown on me that morning. She insisted I shouldn't come that she wanted to go on her own. Are you kidding me, how could I allow my first born and only daughter to go to the hospital all by herself to undergo general anaesthetics? It was non-negotiable. I was going to go.

As I continued the interview, I pulled my jeep up to a curb, and she jumped out and fell on the sidewalk. I jumped out and stood over her while passers-by were looking on wondering what caused the commotion. Many were asking if I wanted help, but I politely declined. Thankfully, my interview ended soon after and I was able to allow her to come back to reality.

It was at this moment that I stood there and also cried to the hospital, as I was so alone with my two kids. It was in this particular experience that I decided I wanted to do this book, the single mothers' diary. It was here I wanted to extend the platform to share, as I knew there had to be more of us out there who struggled as I did.

I didn't just want to share the struggle; I wanted to share God's grace, his mercies and how he carries single mothers such as myself… someone like me who lives in a country with two kids all by myself, one with her mental struggles and the other younger and needing more of my attention.

It was a challenging journey, but his grace was ever sufficient, the hurdles I scaled could only be done with his mercies and favour. So, the Single Mother's Diary was born out of one of lowest points as a single mother myself.

I hope that there will be nuggets here to empower and encourage another single mother on her journey. I wish we didn't have single parent homes but unfortunately, this is inevitable. So whatever skills and tools this book can leave with you to make the journey easier we are all glad to have been a piece of that puzzle for you.

KEY LEARNING

My key takeaways from being a single mother were:

My children were gifts from God, and he entrusted me with them. As a result, I took comfort even in the hardships that he would see me through. I needed to walk away when I was stressed and not take my stress out on my children. I learnt that because a man contributed a sperm doesn't mean that he was committed to be a father. I discovered that I was stronger than I realised I was, and parenting taught me that I had to learn more about my faith in the dark times.

Thank you so much for coming on this journey with us.

Please share your experiences with us, review on Amazon if you can, follow us on social media we will appreciate your support.

Do not forget that we have volume# 2 coming up soon.

To get involved email info@avabrown.org to discuss.

Dr. Ava Eagle Brown – The Mango Girl

Lightning Source UK Ltd.
Milton Keynes UK
UKHW021352031019
350934UK00016B/596/P